LINCOLN, LABOR
AND
SLAVERY

LINCOLN, LABOR

AND

SLAVERY

A CHAPTER

FROM THE

SOCIAL HISTORY OF AMERICA

By

HERMAN SCHLÜTER

NEW YORK

RUSSELL & RUSSELL · INC

1965

FIRST PUBLISHED IN 1913
REISSUED, 1965, BY RUSSELL & RUSSELL, INC.
L. C. CATALOG CARD NO: 65-17920 6-30-67

PRINTED IN THE UNITED STATES OF AMERICA

CONTENTS

CONTENTS

PREFACE

This book has a two-fold purpose: First, to throw light upon the position taken by the working class and the international labor movement regarding chattel slavery; secondly, to indicate the attitude taken by one of the most famous characters in the struggle for the emancipation of the Negro, Abraham Lincoln, towards the labor question and the working class.

The author's standpoint in the treatment of this subject is that of historical materialism, first brought into the science of history by Karl Marx and Friedrich Engels. According to this historical conception the political and intellectual phenomena of history stand in the most intimate relation with the economic and social events in society. It is the economic production, and the division of society into classes caused thereby, which constitutes the foundation of the political and intellectual history of any given epoch. The division of society into classes and their antagonistic interests necessitate the conflict of classes, the *class struggle,* within this society. Feudal, absolutistic, bourgeois and proletarian interests in a given epoch of society become solidified into principles, into ideas of these specific classes, and produce by their contentions with one another universal history. This history offers us the spectacle of a series of struggles which have taken place between the ruled and the ruling, the exploited and the exploiting classes, in the various phases of historical development—struggles from which modern bourgeois society is not exempt.

In our present society class antagonism rests on the exploitation and domination of the working classes, who are deprived of the means of production, by the owners of these means of production, the capitalists. The owners of the soil, of the factories and machinery, of the means of communication, and all other instruments of production, constitute the ruling class precisely *because* they *own* these means of production. The workers constitute the subjected and exploited class precisely *because* they are *excluded from the ownership* of these means of production. These two classes of modern society, the capitalists and the proletarians, or workingmen, are therefore antagonistic to each other alike in their interests and in their ideas. The antagonism of classes naturally produces struggles which, with continued development, will assume larger and larger dimensions. The labor movement and the workingmen's organizations are the expression of these class antagonisms from the side of the working class. Instinctively the workingmen turn against the bourgeois. This class *instinct* changes with increasing antagonism and the greater understanding caused thereby into *class consciousness*. The class struggle assumes greater dimensions and more definite outlines.

We now see what a mistaken notion it is to represent the class consciousness of the workingmen merely as the result of the agitation of labor leaders. It is rather the natural result of social evolution, of the increasing antagonism between the interests of the exploited and the exploiting classes.

It is from the standpoint of this materialistic conception of history that those economic and political questions which the agitation and the struggles in behalf of the emancipation of the Negro slaves brought to the fore, are considered in this book. The position of the early labor movement in relation to the agitation for the abolition of chattel slavery; the economic antagonism between the North and the South and the inevitability of the conflict resulting therefrom, and the position of the international labor movement in relation to the War of Secession, are considered from this point of view—namely, from the standpoint of the working class. The present work is consequently not impartial, does not intend to be impartial. There is indeed no "impartial" history. The historian reflects history as he sees it, and he sees it from the standpoint of the class whose interests he himself represents, whose opinions and ideas he shares, whose struggles are also *his* struggles. The writer of this work takes the position of the most advanced section of the labor movement.

The part which the working class, foreigners as well as Americans, played in the question of Negro slavery and in the struggles resulting therefrom, has never been connectedly treated. And yet this part is well worth the attention of the historian. It is very questionable whether the United States could have passed through the great crisis into which it was thrown by the secession of the Southern States, or could have carried to a victorious finish the tremendous struggle for its existence which ended with the overthrow of chattel slavery, if the working classes of all countries, and the young international labor movement, at that time only beginning, had not helpfully stood by its side.

The United States is indeed under the heaviest obligations to the workingmen, especially to the workingmen of England. The attitude of the

English working class during the gloomiest
period of the North American Republic constitutes one of the brightest pages in the history of
the labor movement. It is a subject which has
not only not received the attention it deserves
at the hands of bourgeois historians, but has
even been deliberately ignored by them.

Thus it happens, that even in the ranks of the
American labor movement but few are aware that
the United States probably owes its existence to
the attitude of the working class of England.
For it was the *working class,* and the working
class *only,* which then opposed in England the war
which the ruling classes of that country, with the
Government at their head, were about to declare
in favor of the seceding Southern States against
the Northern States of the Union. It was the
working class of England which, under the guid-
ance of leaders, the best that ever stood at the
head of the English labor movement, through its
determined attitude prevented the intended war,
a war which would have added enormously to the
perils by which at that time the United States
was surrounded. The representatives of the Government at Washington spoke indeed only of the
"popular sentiment" in England in favor of the
North. They were ignorant of the division of
classes in society, and they failed to perceive that
it was the English *working class* which backed
this "popular sentiment," and that this class divi-

sion was the cause of the workingmen taking sides against the ruling class of their country, because the continuance of unfree labor was an obstacle in the path of the development of free labor.

Among the few in Washington who at that time recognized the fact that it was the workingmen of England, and these *only,* who stood behind the "popular sentiment" in favor of the North, was Abraham Lincoln. In his answer to an address of the workingmen of Manchester he declared the attitude of the English working class on the question of Negro slavery, to be "an instance of sublime Christian heroism which has not been surpassed in any age or in any country."

Lincoln's keener insight in this case does not prove that he was equally clear-sighted in the matter of the labor movement and all that it implies, or that he arrived at a clear understanding of it. His public utterances in regard to his position toward the working class, as well as in regard to his views on the labor movement, reveal no special clarity. He did not recognize the significance of the labor movement and its struggles; he could not recognize it. In his time the American labor movement was still in its infancy. Only in the Eastern section of the country, where manufacture had begun to develop, could its beginning be discerned. Lincoln himself did not come into touch with the American labor movement, at least not into close touch, and it was therefore perfectly explicable why he could not reach definite conclusions concerning the aims of this movement, its tasks and the economic causes which gave rise to it.

In the present work the author has attempted to determine Lincoln's position toward the working class. In this attempt he has examined all the documents and speeches of Lincoln relating to workingmen. If it should appear that Lincoln was not a man who arrived at clear views in regard to the labor movement and to a knowledge of its causes, no reproach is thereby intended. He was not a member of the class of industrial workers, but a representative of the lower middle class (known in Europe as the *petit bourgeoisie*), which in conjunction with the farmers constituted the majority of the inhabitants of the United States in his time. He championed the interests of this middle class and could not rise above its opinions. And how small was the effect which the labor movement made on public opinion in the United States prior to the Civil War!

In the statement of his subject the author has preferred not only to support his assertions by reference to documentary evidence, but to a great extent to let these documents speak for themselves. The coherence of the narrative may occasionally suffer by reason of the use of so many quotations; but as many of these documents are rare and comparatively inaccessible, it has been thought best to reproduce thèm.

The author is indebted to Mr. Algernon Lee and Mr. W. J. Ghent for their careful reading of the manuscript.

HERMAN SCHLÜTER.

New York, Summer of 1913.

CHAPTER I.

ECONOMIC ANTAGONISM AND POLITICAL STRUGGLE.

1. HISTORICAL REVIEW.

Long before a bloody civil war put an end to chattel slavery in the United States, this social institution was the source of all kinds of economic antagonisms which found expression in the political life of the nation. Our ante-bellum political and economic history can be understood only by a consideration of Negro slavery and all pertaining to it, even in the judgment of questions which were not directly related to it.

The entire domestic and foreign policy of the United States in the first half of the last century was defined in all its contents through slavery. The opposing interests which were created through the existence of slavery brought about that movement and that conflict within the ruling classes of the country which finally led to civil war. What came to be decided in this Civil War was not so much the question whether people within the United States should be held as slaves on account of the color of their skin, as the question whether the interests of the slaveholders of the South or the interests of the industrialists and manufacturers of the North should have the deciding voice in the shaping of our national life.

In the South the prevailing mode of production was slavery, unfree labor. The Southern proprietors of plantations produced their staples—tobacco, cotton, rice, sugar—by means of Negroes who were their personal property, whom consequently they were obliged to feed and clothe, but to whom they did not have to pay money wages. In the North, especially after the second war with England (1812-1815), industries developed which employed "free" laborers—laborers who did not sell themselves and their entire time, but only their labor power during certain hours to their employers for wages. The struggles resulting from these antagonisms, which in the main were struggles waged for political supremacy in the Union, constitute the contents of the political development which led to the abolition of slavery.

Changed economic conditions produce a change in the opinions and ideas of men. As long as the possessing classes of New England had an interest in Negro slavery, they manifested no hostility to this institution. As long as the ships of the New Englanders, laden with rum made in New England, sailed to Africa and there exchanged their rum for Negro slaves, whom they carried to the Southern States to exchange for molasses, which in turn they took to New England, where rum was made out of it; as long as this circle—rum, Negroes, molasses, rum—remained and proved to be profitable, so long few voices were heard in New England demanding the abolition of slavery.

All this was changed when modern industry began to develop. There were cotton factories in New England as early as 1790, but it was the second war with England which carried them to prosperity. By the interruption of its commerce with England the United States was cut off from its source of supplies and thrown upon its own resources. The increased demand gave a powerful impetus to cotton and woolen manufacture. And although with the advent of peace the English commodity regained its former advantage, industry continued to develop in New England, entailing antagonisms of various sorts between its interests and the interests of the slaveholders, the planters of the South. The idea of the abolition of slavery arose in New England.

In the South, also, a change in economic interests was accomplished by a change in the opinions of men. In the Border slave states—in Virginia, for instance—there arose in the latter part of the eighteenth century ideas and movements aiming at the mitigation or abolition of slavery. Rapacious tillage and the exhaustion of the soil incident thereto, peculiar to slave labor, led to a condition of the tobacco plantations which made their further cultivation unprofitable. People began to feel the possession of slaves as a burden, and in consequence became philanthropically inclined. We see this demonstrated by the fact, for instance, that the South, and especially Virginia, sent delegates to the annual Abolitionist conventions in Philadelphia, which had their inception in New England. But this practice ceased when slavery suddenly again became profitable. Philanthropy went to the devil when money poured into the cash-box.

Meanwhile in 1803, the United States had purchased from France the extensive territory which was at that time known as Louisiana. The sugar and rice fields of the new territory created a market for Negro slaves, the demands of which could hardly be satisfied. The planters of the Border slave States, to whom the cultivation of tobacco had become unprofitable and who for climatic reasons could not think of raising cotton, now threw themselves into the production of Negro slaves, into the "manufacture" of Negroes. They bred Negroes, as cattle are bred, and sold them to the planters of the cotton and sugar States. With the increased interest in Negro slavery in Virginia philanthropy disappeared, and nothing further was heard there in regard to the abolition of slavery. But voices began to be raised in favor of the abolition of the slave *trade*. New England ships carrying slaves from the coast of Africa to America offered a sharp competition to the Virginia planters who bred Negroes on American soil. As early as 1808 the slave trade was legally prohibited. Notwithstanding this prohibition the ship owners of the North, and especially of New York, continued to carry on the trade briskly, and it was still active as late as the beginning of the sixties.

These and other antagonistic interests between the ruling classes of American society, between the manufacturers of the North and the planters of the South, gave rise to the later movement for the abolition of slavery, a movement which first manifested itself in the formation of Abolitionist societies. These societies originated in the beginning of the thirties in the large cities of the North, especially in Boston, after an earlier movement by the same name and with the same ends had completely ceased to exist. While the earlier Abolitionists had fought slavery with the Bible in their hands, the new movement forged additional weapons for itself out of political economy and statistics, and from economic considerations demonstrated the necessity for the abolition of slave labor. These Abolitionists were untiring in demanding immediate abolition. Although they were very weak in the beginning, they nevertheless accomplished wonders by the agitation among the masses coincident with the in-

creasing antagonism of interests between the
North and the South.

2. Economic Contrast.

Economic antagonism between the North and
the South had for a long time found political expression in tariff legislation. The capitalists of
the North, who paid their free laborers wages,
were interested in legislation which depressed
wages and raised the price of commodities. The
Southern slaveholders, on the other hand, sought
to purchase cheaply the supplies which they required for the support of their numerous slaves
and for the operation of their plantations, and
they consequently advocated such legislation as
promised to depress the prices of these supplies
to the lowest possible level. We thus observe in
the North tendencies aiming at a protective tariff.
Its infant industries could be protected against
foreign competition only by a high tariff. The
protective system which "manufactures" manufacturers by creating high prices for manufactured goods, was for this very reason abhorred
by the South. We consequently find there the
most ardent champions of free trade.

Slavery precluded all industrial development,
as well as all agriculture on a scientific and economical basis, and was restricted exclusively to the
cultivation of staple articles. The prime staple
was cotton, the cultivation of which admitted of

the application of human labor power in its most primitive form and by means of the most primitive tools. The cotton planter knew but one interest—namely, to sell his cotton at high prices and to buy his supplies at the lowest possible prices.

Slave labor became profitable only when the planter gave his undivided attention to cotton. The less grain and food products he produced, the larger was his harvest of cotton, the greater his profit. The cheaper he purchased his provisions, the cheaper could he produce his cotton, and the larger was his profit. If he had undertaken to raise his own grain, he would hardly have been in a position to produce enough cotton for export. The Northern and Western farmer consequently worked for the South, by sending the surplus of his grain there. But he demanded good prices for his products, while the planter was willing to pay but little, and so the former was brought into further antagonism with the South.

The fact of the predominance of protective-tariff sentiments in the North and of free-trade sentiments in the South did not preclude opposition to these tendencies on the part of certain groups of interests within those sections. Thus, in the North, the commercial element of the large cities, especially of New York, as well as the ship-owners, were pronounced free traders and in turn supporters of slavery, while the sugar planters of the South advocated a high tariff.

The conflict between the two tendencies in tariff legislation dates back to the year 1828. In that year the manufacturers favoring a protective tariff succeeded for the first time in passing a tariff law which was wholly dictated by a regard for the development of industrial enterprise. Before that tariffs had been levied mainly for revenue, with a regard to meeting the expenses of government. The first attempt to inaugurate a protective policy created a storm of dissent in the South and led to a fierce struggle against it. Beginning with 1833 one duty after another was abolished, until in 1857, after many changes in tariff legislation, the Democrats in Congress succeeded in passing a tariff schedule with lower duties than the Union had known since 1812.

The South was connected with England by a bond of common interest. The rapidly developing textile industries of Great Britain were in great need of the raw cotton of the South, which possessed a monopoly in its production. As return freight the cotton ships brought back England's industrial products, which became cheaper and cheaper, and which came into the country unchecked by the prevailing tariff. England's competition became more and more oppressive to Northern industry. The antagonism between the capital which employed free labor in the North

and the capital which employed slave labor in the
South became more and more pronounced, and a
serious clash seemed inevitable.

We must mention one more fact which intensified the antagonism between the farmers of the
North and West and the planters of the South.
Slave labor and plantation farming led to a rapid
deterioration and exhaustion of the soil. The
slaveholders were therefore in constant need of
new territory for exploitation and devastation.
Hence the endeavors of the South to acquire new
territory and to make slavery there a legal institution. The economic life, and consequently the
political predominance of the South in the Union,
lay in the extension of cotton culture. If the
South lost the power of expansion, it lost the possibility of existence. This fact explains the virul-
ence of the slaveholders whenever the question of
the extension of slave territory came up for debate. Therefore the interminable intrigues which
in the thirties and forties led first to the independence and then to the annexation of Texas
Therefore the Mexican War and the extension of
the territory of the United States to include Cali-
fornia, Utah and New Mexico. Therefore also
the various expeditions to Cuba in order to acquire this island for the South. Therefore even
the invasion of Central America, of which it was
frankly said that the aim of its promoters was
the restoration of slavery, which had been abol-

ished there.   Therefore especially also the attempt to make of slavery a legal institution in all those States of the Union which were suitable for the production of cotton or of slaves.

But these attempts aiming at the seizure of the still extant virgin soil in behalf of slave labor were at war with the interests of the farmer of the North and the West.   The farmer, also, was greatly interested in new territory.   Often enough he left his old homestead in search of new virgin soil.   But there was no place for the labor of the free farmer where slave labor prevailed, and the competitive struggles between him and the planter, especially in the border territory between the free and slave states, formed an additional reason for him to take a stand against slavery. It was in the main pre-eminently the farmer element, too, which took the field for the preservation of the Union and the subjugation of the insurgent South.

3. POLITICAL STRUGGLE.

In Congress the Southerners spent all their energy in efforts to establish their dominion.   In August, 1850, the Fugitive Law was passed, which empowered every slave holder to pursue and seize fugitive slaves throughout the whole Union, including the free states, where slavery did not exist.   By this law the very sovereignty of the Northern States was abolished.   Another

measure of the Compromise of 1850 permitted
the first extension of slavery over new territory
(New Mexico and Utah). This was followed by
the Kansas-Nebraska Bill (1854) which deprived Congress of the power of prohibiting slavery anywhere, but left the decision to the individual States and practically opened the entire
West to the introduction of slavery. Then came
the bloody encounters between the free-State
people and the adherents of slavery in Kansas.
The Dred Scott decision of 1857 followed. It
was these questions almost exclusively which
dominated the internal policy of the country and
determined the formation of new parties.

The Republican party was formed in 1854 by
the progressive elements of the Democratic and
the old Whig parties and the Free Soilers. It was
opposed to slavery, but its opposition was directed
far more against the extension of slavery than
against the institution itself. Its slogan was not
originally the abolition of slavery, but rather:
No more Slave States. As late as 1856 a radical
paper hostile to slavery complained of the Republicans: "Everywhere bargains, compromises,
concessions which make it almost impossible for
an honest man to participate in the struggle!"

How little the Republican party originally
thought of demanding complete abolition is made
plain by a glance at the platform which was
adopted by its first general convention at Phila-

delphia, in 1856. The planks which in this platform referred to slavery were: First, opposition
to the introduction of slavery into the Territories,
so that neither Congress, nor the Territorial Legislature, nor any company or individual should
have the right under the prevailing constitution
to legalize slavery there; and, further, an assertion of the constitutional power and obligation of
Congress to prohibit slavery and polygamy in the
Territories. Absolutely nothing was said in behalf of the abolition of slavery itself in the slave
States.

Even in 1860, when a violent conflict already
seemed inevitable; when the proceedings in Congress had carried the political antagonisms to an
acute stage; when John Brown's attempted insurrection and his death on the gallows had set
the population in both camps aflame with excitement—even then the Republicans did not demand
abolition. In their convention of that year at
Chicago, in which Abraham Lincoln was nomi-
nated for the Presidency, a new platform was
adopted, containing, among others, these planks
in regard to slavery:

"That the new dogma, that the Constitution,
of its own force, carries slavery into any or all
of the Territories of the United States, is a dangerous political heresy, at variance with the explicit provisions of that instrument itself, with
contemporaneous exposition, and with legislative

and judicial precedent; is revolutionary in its tendency and subversive of the peace and harmony of the country.

"That the normal condition of all the territory of the United States is that of freedom; that as our republican fathers, when they had abolished slavery in all our national territory, ordained that 'no person should be deprived of life, liberty or property without due process of law,' it becomes our duty, by legislation, whenever such legislation is necessary, to maintain this provision of the Constitution against all attempts to violate it; and we deny the authority of Congress, of a Territorial Legislature, or of any individuals, to give legal existence to slavery in any Territory of the United States.

"That we brand the recent reopening of the African slave trade, under the cover of our national flag, aided by perversions of judicial power, as a crime against humanity and a burning shame to our country and age, and we call upon Congress to take prompt and efficient measures for the total and final suppression of that execrable traffic."

Thus we see that on the very eve of the outbreak of hostilities between the North and the South the Republicans were silent in regard to abolition. They contented themselves with protesting against the extension of the institution over Federal territory and with condemning the slave *trade,* which had been reopened. They still had no objections to urge against slavery itself, or at least they did not consider it expedient to place the demand for abolition in the foreground.

In the Fall of 1860, Abraham Lincoln was elected to the Presidency of the United States. The South unfurled the flag of rebellion. Futile attempts to effect a compromise were still made in Congress, and the Republicans, in order to save the union, showed a willingness to concede much of what they had previously stood for. But with the outbreak of hostilities the attitude of the Republican leaders gradually became more radical, though the necessity of conciliating a large part of the population in the Border States compelled the utmost caution. No one better understood the necessity of this caution than Lincoln; and from time to time he had to withstand bursts of angry impatience from sections of the Northern people who insisted upon a more radical attitude.

Lincoln's position in regard to secession and slavery during the early part of the war, and the position of the radicals and the Abolitionists in regard to Lincoln and the Republican Administration is brought out most clearly in a controversy on the subject between Lincoln and Horace Greeley, the Abolitionist editor of the New York *Tribune.* In August, 1862, Greeley published in the New York *Tribune* an open letter addressed to Lincoln. His appeal to the President was entitled "The Prayer of Twenty Millions," and in the course of it he requested Lincoln to write to the United States Ministers in Europe and ask them "to tell you [Lincoln] candidly, whether the seeming subserviency of your policy to the slave-holding, slavery-upholding interest, is not the perplexity, the despair of statesmen and of parties, and be admonished by the general answer!"

Lincoln replied to this public appeal of Horace Greeley as follows:

"Executive Mansion, Washington.
"August 22, 1862.

"Hon. Horace Greeley:

"Dear Sir: I have just read yours of the 19th, addressed to myself through the New York *Tribune*. If there be in it statements or assumptions of fact which I may know to be erroneous, I do not now and here controvert them. If there be in it any inferences which I may believe to be falsely drawn, I do not now and here argue against them. If there be perceptible in it an impatient and dictatorial tone, I waive it in deference to an old friend, whose heart I have always supposed to be right.

"As to the policy I 'seem to be pursuing,' as you say, I have not meant to leave any one in doubt.

"I would save the Union. I would save it the shortest way under the Constitution. The sooner

the national authority can be restored, the nearer
the Union will be 'the Union as it was.' If there
be those who would not save the Union unless
they could at the same time save slavery, I do
not agree with them. If there be those who
would not save the Union unless they could at
the same time destroy slavery, I do not agree
with them. My paramount object in this struggle
is to save the Union, and is not either to save or
destroy slavery. If I could save the Union without freeing any slaves, I would do it; and if I
could save it by freeing all the slaves, I would do
it; and if I could do it by freeing some and leaving
others alone, I would also do that. What I do
about slavery and the colored race, I do because I
believe it helps to save this Union; and what I
forbear doing, I forbear because I do not believe
it would help to save the Union. I shall do less
whenever I shall believe what I am doing hurts
the cause, and I shall do more whenever I shall
believe doing more will help the cause. I shall
try to correct errors when shown to be errors;
and I shall adopt new views so fast as they shall
appear to be true views. I have here stated my
purpose according to my views of official duty,
and I intend no modification of my oft expressed
personal wish that all men, everywhere, could
be free.

"Yours,

"A. Lincoln."

Horace Greeley published a reply, in which he raised the question whether Lincoln intended to save the Union "by recognizing, obeying, and enforcing the laws, or by ignoring, disregarding and in fact defying them."

Greeley's answer to this question was as follows:

"I stand upon the law of the land. The humblest has a clear right to invoke its protection and support against even the highest. That law—in strict accordance with the law of nations, of Nature and of God—declares that every traitor now engaged in the infernal work of destroying our country has forfeited thereby all claims or color of right lawfully to hold human beings in slavery. I ask of you a clear and public recognition that this law is to be obeyed wherever the national authority is respected. I cite to you instances wherein men fleeing from bondage to traitors, to the protection of our flag, have been assaulted, wounded, and murdered by soldiers of the Union, unpunished and unrebuked by your General Commanding,—to prove that it is your duty to take action in the premises,—action that will cause the law to be proclaimed and obeyed wherever your authority or that of the Union is recognized as paramount. The Rebellion is strengthened, the national cause is imperilled, by every hour's delay to strike treason this staggering blow.

"When Frémont proclaimed freedom to the

slaves of rebels, you constrained him to modify
his proclamation into rigid accordance with the
terms of the existing law. It was your clear
right to do so. I now ask of you conformity to
the principle so sternly enforced upon him. I
ask you to instruct your generals and com-
modores, that no loyal person—certainly none
willing to render service to the national cause—
is henceforth to be regarded as the slave of any
traitor. While no rightful government was ever
before assailed by so wanton and wicked a rebellion as that of the slaveholders against our national life, I am sure none ever before hesitated at so
simple and primary an act of self-defence, as to
relieve those who would serve and save it from
chattel servitude to those who are wading through
seas of blood to subvert and destroy it. Future
generations will with difficulty realize that there
could have been hesitation on this point. Sixty
years of general and boundless subserviency to
the slave power do not adequately explain it.

"Mr. President, I beseech you to open your
eyes to the fact that the devotees of slavery everywhere—just as much in Maryland as in Missis-
sippi, in Washington as in Richmond—are to-
day your enemies, and the implacable foes of
every effort to re-establish the national authority
by the discomfiture of its assailants. Their President is not Abraham Lincoln, but Jefferson Davis.
You may draft them to serve in the war; but they

will only fight under the Rebel flag. There is not in New York to-day a man who really believes in slavery, loves it, and desires its perpetuation, who heartily desires the crushing out of the Rebellion. He would much rather save the Republic by buying up and pensioning off its assailants. His 'Union as it was' is a Union of which you were not President, and no one who truly wished freedom to all, ever could be.

"If these are truths, Mr. President, they are surely of the gravest importance. You cannot safely approach the great and good end you so intently meditate by shutting your eyes to them. Your deadly foe is not blinded by any mist in which *your* eyes may be developed. He walks straight to his goal, knowing well his weak point, and most unwillingly betraying his fear that you too may see and take advantage of it. God grant that apprehension may prove prophetic!

"That you may reasonably perceive these vital truths as they will shine forth on the pages of history,—that they may be read by our children irradiated by the glory of our national salvation, not rendered lurid by the blood-red glow of national conflagration and ruin—that you may promptly and practically realize that slavery is to be vanquished only by liberty,—is the fervent and anxious prayer of

"Yours truly,

"Horace Greeley."

The attitude of the Administration and of Congress toward slavery, though cautious, was steadily progressive. In August, 1861, Congress passed a Confiscation act, freeing slaves who were directly employed in aiding the Confederate cause. Gen. John C. Frémont, in command in Missouri, soon after issued a proclamation exceeding the terms of this act in that it freed the slaves of all persons in rebellion against the Government. Lincoln immediately disallowed the proclamation and soon after (November 2d) removed Frémont. Gen. B. F. Butler, however, was not interfered with for treating the slaves in the Fort Monroe neighborhood as "contraband of war." In March, 1862, Lincoln sent a message to Congress advocating the gradual abolition of slavery, with compensation, but the measure failed. In the following month Congress abolished slavery in the District of Columbia, and an average compensation of $200 per slave was paid. In June Congress abolished slavery in the Territories, granting no compensation; and in July the Confiscation act was extended and strengthened. On July 22d Lincoln read the first draft of his Emancipation Proclamation to his cabinet, but decided to withhold it until a decisive victory had been gained. Shortly afterward Gen. David Hunter, in command in South Carolina, issued a proclamation as sweeping as the one issued a year before by Gen. Frémont.

This, also, was disallowed by Lincoln, though within a few weeks (September 22d) he issued his own proclamation. On January 1, 1863, this proclamation went into effect. On February 1, 1865, by a two-thirds majority, Congress passed the Thirteenth Amendment, and on December 18th it was officially proclaimed as having been ratified by a sufficient number of States.

CHAPTER II.

THE WORKINGMEN AND CHATTEL SLAVERY.

1. THE INDUSTRIAL WORKERS OF THE NORTH AND SLAVERY.

The whole course of development sketched in the foregoing chapter—the inception and rise of the movement in behalf of the emancipation of the Negro slaves, the economic and political antagonisms and struggles engendered by slavery, the formation of new political parties, and finally the attempt to disrupt the Union—this whole course of development was accompanied by, and stood in the most intimate relation with, another economic phenomenon—namely, the rise of capitalist industry in the North and the concomitant growth of an industrial working class with separate class interests and separate class feelings, developing into perfect class consciousness with the advent of greater intelligence.

Now, what position did these industrial workers of the North take regarding chattel slavery? It was in the nature of things that slavery and free labor could not peaceably continue to exist side by side. The intelligence and the class consciousness of the free workingmen may not have been sufficiently developed than to apprehend the economic reasons which preclude the co-existence of slave labor and free labor, and the workingmen may especially not have been able to see that their own development as a class was imperiled by slavery, but their class feeling was certainly far enough advanced to dispose them in most cases against the existence of slavery. This attitude, however, was originally less the result of a clear apprehension than of the emanation of a certain feeling, which again and again, as we shall see, was traversed by their own class interest, and which gave to the position of the workingmen in regard to Negro slavery a strangely contradictory aspect.

Previous to the Civil War in America but few countries knew anything about the labor movement and labor organization. Only in England and in the United States was there a working class with separate class interests sufficiently developed to admit of its organization and mobilization as an independent class.

At the beginning of the nineteenth century trade unions had begun to appear in England. In the thirties and forties the British proletariat had created for itself a vigorous political labor organization in the Chartist movement. In Germany, France and the other European countries the workingmen had not got beyond the first attempts at organization and were as yet without any idea of an independent labor movement. It was not to be expected therefore that the Continental workingman would take an independent position in regard to Negro slavery.

In the United States the first trade organizations of workingmen had made their appearance simultaneously with the formation of trade unions in England. As early as the latter part of the twenties and the beginning of the thirties we note also the formation of independent political labor organizations, but all of short duration. The development of the trade-union movement was again and again interrupted by the economic crises of the ante-bellum period, especially those of 1837 and 1857, and the existing organizations were destroyed. The political labor parties also soon disappeared: wrecked partly by the incomplete development of conditions and partly by the intrigues of professional politicians and the corruption of the labor leaders. Nevertheless new organizations and new movements started into life again. The more industry developed, the more numerous became the attempts of workingmen to found independent organizations.

Corresponding with the development of industry, the American labor movement of that period was restricted to the Northern States, especially to the Eastern portion. New England, New York, Philadelphia and Baltimore were the prin-

cipal seats of activity. In the South single associations of mechanics, especially printers, shipwrights, and iron moulders, were indeed formed
in the fifties, but in general they were of little
account. The entire West was devoted to agriculture and consequently offered but little soil for
the growth of an industrial labor movement.

In the Eastern portion of the country, especially in New York, the German immigrant workingmen played a part. Many trades were almost
exclusively in the hands of skilled German artisans. They organized independent unions for
the promotion of their own interests, and in the
middle of the forties there arose a German labor
movement on American soil, which frequently
exerted great influence. In determining the position of the labor movement in regard to Negro
slavery only England and the United States are
consequently to be considered, and in the latter
country the attitude of the immigrant German
workingmen must be taken into account along
with that of the native organizations.

Through the agitation of the Abolitionists,
which was vigorously supported by the social reformers of the Fourier and Owen schools and by
the men and women interested in Brook Farm,
who exercised a great influence upon the workingmen, the industrial laborers and artisans of
New England became early enlightened with regard to slavery, and they took position accord-

ingly. Their attitude on this matter furnishes another proof that the salvation of the world does not proceed from the palaces, but comes from the hovels; and that it is the despised and lower strata of society in which all reformatory movements, which together constitute the progress of mankind, strike root and have their soil.

The strong hold which the teachings of the Abolitionists gained among the mass of the workingmen of New England, and the coldness with which these teachings were received by the upper ten of society, are facts attested by an eye-witness who himself sprang from the latter class. Thomas Wentworth Higginson, a native of New England, writes of the early thirties of the last century, after William Lloyd Garrison had launched his Abolitionist agitation and founded the *Liberator* in Boston:

"The anti-slavery movement was not strongest in the more educated classes, but was predominantly a people's movement, based on the simplest human instincts and far stronger for a time in the factories and shoe-shops than in the pulpits or colleges."

And further:

"All of us were familiar with the vain efforts of Garrison to enlist the clergy in the anti-slavery cause, and Stephen Foster, one of the stanchest of the early Abolitionists, habitually spoke of them as the 'Brotherhood of Thieves.' Lawyers

and doctors, too, fared hard with those enthusi-
asts. and merchants not much better."*

Thus we see it was the working class, and not
the property owners of New England, that list-
ened to the Abolitionists. And like the unorgan-
ized mass of the workingmen of the North, so
also the first organized workingmen showed an
understanding of the question of Negro slavery
and sympathized with the Abolitionists in their
efforts to abolish the institution. The platform
of one of the first political labor parties of New
York contained a plank demanding the abolition
of chattel slavery; and as an expression of their
own class interest, they demanded at the same
time the abolition of wage slavery, a term which
had far greater currency in the American labor
movement at that period than subsequently.

The question of the abolition of wage slavery,
as well as the demands of the labor movement in
general, met with far less understanding among
the Abolitionists than the question of the abolition of chattel slavery among the workingmen.
The Abolitionists denied the very existence of
"white slavery." They opposed the spokesmen
of the workingmen who in their speeches and
articles used the term "white slavery," and flatly
denied that wage workers were slaves. The
Abolitionists, indeed, evinced so little understand-

---

* Thomas Wentworth Higginson: *Cheerful Yester-
days.* 1898. pp. 115-117.

ing of the rising movement of the workingmen that they denied them the right of independent organization, of making separate demands as a class, and of securing their special interests.

On January 1, 1831, there appeared in Boston the first number of the *Liberator,* the organ of the Abolitionists, which William Lloyd Garrison published for thirty years in the interest of the emancipation of the Negro slaves. The same time saw the birth of a movement for the purpose of organizing the workingmen of New England into an independent political labor party. This labor party was founded in a convention held at Boston in February, 1831, under the name "New England Association of Farmers, Mechanics and other Workingmen." In the first issue of the *Liberator* William Lloyd Garrison opposed the agitation in behalf of this independent labor party in the following words:

"An attempt has been made—it is still making—we regret to say, with considerable success —to inflame the minds of our working classes against the more opulent, and to persuade men that they are contemned and oppressed by a wealthy aristocracy. That public grievances exist, is unquestionably true; but they are not confined to any one class of society. Every profession is interested in their removal—the rich as well as the poor. It is in the highest degree criminal, therefore, to exasperate our mechanics to

deeds of violence or to array them under a party
banner; for it is not true, that, at any time, they
have been the objects of reproach. Labor is not
dishonorable. The industrious artisan, in a government like ours, will always be held in better
estimation than the wealthy idler.

"Our limits will not allow us to enlarge on this
subject; we may return to it another time. We
are the friends of reform; but this is not reform,
which in one evil threatens to inflict a thousand
others."

The hostile attitude of Garrison and a portion
of the other Abolitionists toward the labor movement very naturally put a damper on the enthusiasm of the workingmen, especially the organized workmen, for the Abolitionists' movement.
In their meetings, conventions, and newspapers
the workingmen set forth more strongly than
ever the slave character of wage labor, but continued as a matter of course to champion the
emancipation of the Negro slaves, without, however, emphasizing its immediate necessity. A
spokesman of the Boston workingmen, probably
William West, combated Garrison's views in the
columns of the *Liberator* itself. In a communication to this paper he described the condition of
the wage worker and addressed Garrison in the
following manner:

"Although you do not appear to have per-
ceived it, I think there is a very intimate connec-

tion between the interests of the workingmen's
party and your own. You are striving to excite
the attention of your countrymen to the injustice
of holding their fellow-men in bondage and de-
priving them of the fruit of their toil. We are
aiming at a similar object, only in application to
another portion of our fellow-men."

West then discusses the causes which in his
opinion bring about the slavery of white workingmen, saying among other things that "the
value and the prices of labor have been rated not
by the *worth* of *their product,* but by the *power*
of those who command its proceeds, or for whom
it is performed to *obtain* it, and enjoy its benefits." . . . .

And then West continues:

"You propose to remedy these evils, by extending to the enslaved the sympathy of the philanthropic, by educating and otherwise fitting them
to take care of themselves; and by awakening the
moral sense of those who now enjoy the fruit of
their labors, to the injustice and wickedness of
thus robbing their fellow-men of the products
of their industrial toil.

"We seek to enlighten our brethren in the
knowledge of their rights and duties; to excite
them to the acquisition of useful knowledge and
the practice of virtue; and to cherish that self-
respect which they are entitled to feel, who support all other classes of society. *We,* too, appeal

to the moral sense of the wealthy and powerful, and to their justice and philanthropy, in behalf of those whose labor give value to their estates— income to their capital—ornament and beauty to their dwellings and apartments. We demand of these, that they should pay to the hard-working farmer and mechanic, not only a fair equivalent for his services, but that homage and respect which are due to him who braves the inclemency of winter and the intensity of summer; who toils early and late to raise up into life a virtuous family. We insist that where reason and argument will not avail, it is a duty owned by workingmen to themselves and the world, to exert their power, through the ballot-box,—and by ameliorating our system of Laws, to eradicate those evils which operate so extensively and unjustly."

The discussion between the Abolitionist and that Boston workman went on through several numbers of the *Liberator*. On January 29, 1831, Garrison answered West and told him, that "there is a prevalent opinion that wealth and aristocracy are indissolubly allied; and the poor and vulgar are taught to consider the opulent as their natural enemies. Those who inculcate this pernicious doctrine are the worst enemies of the people, and in grain, the real nobility. There is, no doubt, an abuse of wealth as well as of talents, office and emolument; but where is the evidence that our wealthy citizens, as a body, are hostile to the interests of the laboring classes? It is not found in their commercial enterprises, which whiten the ocean with canvas, and give employment to the useful and numerous class of men: it is not found in their manufacturing establishments, which multiply labor and cheapen the necessities of the poor; it is not found in the luxuries of their tables, or the adornments of their dwellings, for which they must pay in proportion to their extravagance.

"It is a miserable characteristic of human nature to look with an envious eye upon those who are more fortunate in their pursuits, or more exalted in their station. In every grade, there are unprincipled, avaricious and despotic men: but shall individual cases condemn the whole body? Perhaps it would be nearer the truth to affirm, that mechanics are more inimical to the success of each other, more unjust toward each other, than the rich toward them."

As we see, Garrison did not penetrate to the kernel of the matter. He simply had no understanding for the point of view of his adversary, who even at that time, more than eighty years ago, rose far above the level of the mass of the American workingmen of the present day as regards a true conception of the labor question.

West replied once more to Garrison's rejoinder, in these words:

"You must concede that those who indulge in luxury, are in no sense more deserving than the working classes who live frugally and in republican simplicity. But do we see the latter enjoying the advantages of the former? Where do you find the men whose toil and labor have produced all the magnificence and grandeur which adorn our capital? Living in the poorest hovels, or meanest dwellings—subsisting on the humblest fare—working in all weather, exposed to every evil—and enjoying but little leisure or opportunity for the cultivation of heart or intellect. Would this be so, if they were equitably paid for their labor? Is it not obvious that the prices of mechanical and agricultural labor are altogether too low, when an idle libertine, who *produces nothing,* can command the proceeds of the labor of all around him, and live at the cost which would support a hundred industrious working citizens and their useful families? I am persuaded that a moment's reflection on this subject must satisfy you, that labor is altogether inadequately compensated. The very existence of such accumulations is proof of it."

The antagonism revealed in this controversy between the spokesman of the Abolitionists and the champion of the workingmen found expression during the whole period of the Abolitionist movement whenever the workingman, in their meetings or in their papers, had occasion to define their position in regard to Negro slavery. It would be a mistake, therefore, to assume that Garrison's attack upon the labor movement was the sole cause of the estrangement existing between the two movements, an estrangement evidenced among other things by the fact that the workingmen very seldom expressed an opinion about the efforts for the abolishment of Negro slavery and that the Abolitionists reported very little about the labor movement. The attitude of the organized workingmen towards Southern slavery had a deeper cause. As already stated, this cause lay in their awakening class consciousness. This indeed did not dispose the workingmen against the emancipation of the Negro slaves. *but it suggested to them that their own emancipation was a matter of more vital importance to them than that of the Southern blacks.* Their feelings and their sympathies in general aligned them indeed on the side of the agitation in behalf of the abolition of Negro slavery; but with their awakening understanding and their dawning insight into their own lot the conviction grew within them that their own emancipation touched them more nearly. While the great mass of the unorganized workingmen of New England thus furnished the great body whence the Abolitionists drew their recruits, there came a reaction with the rise of the labor movement and the formation of independent organizations by workingmen, whether political parties or trade unions. In the labor organizations the specific demands of labor and the class feeling were naturally more sharply emphasized than among the unorganized masses. This fact explains also why the agitation in behalf of the abolition of Negro slavery met with less response among the organized work-ingmen of that period than among the unorgan-ized masses. Though the hostility of the Abo-litionists may have widened the breach, yet their own affairs, their own struggles, and their own agitation—in short, the awakening class con-sciousness of the workingmen—made of the abo-lition of Southern Negro slavery a matter of sec-ondary importance to them. We come face to face with this fact again and again. Labor or-ganizations at that time were not yet well estab-lished institutions. Crises and accidents of all sorts too often put an end to them. But they always rose afresh, and in the three decades pre-ceding the Civil War we note again and again the fact that with the rise of the new organization the question of Negro slavery gives way to the question of wage slavery.

There is also to be noted among the working-men of that period a certain natural suspicion which is wont to go with every genuine labor-class movement when it must declare itself in reference to middle-class reform. For instance, when, in the Fall of 1835, Governor Vroom, of

New York, in a message to the Legislature, made an attack on the Abolitionists, the *Workingmen's Advocate* then published in New York, declared:

"We believe that many of the Abolitionists are actuated by a species of fanaticism, and are desirous of freeing the slaves, *more* for the purpose of adding them to a religious sect, than for a love of liberty and justice, but their desire to *free* the slaves, so far as they can do so by the force of moral power, we believe to be a good and a just cause, and one that they have not attempted to advance by any but constitutional means."*

At that period, especially in New England, the disciples of Fourier and Robert Owen and other utopian social reformers, who had inaugurated a great movement throughout the United States. exercised a powerful influence on the ideas and opinions of the workingmen. The men and women participating in this movement, especially also those interested in the Brook Farm experiment, not only exercised great influence upon the workingmen, but they were also in close touch with the Abolitionists and they promoted the anti-slavery cause with great energy. Whatever school they might belong to, all these social reformers agreed with the organized workingmen on the question of Negro slavery, although they took a livelier interest than did the workingmen

---

* *Working Men's Advocate,* New York, Nov. 21, 1835.

in the special work of the Abolitionists. In the *Liberator,* as well as in the numerous anti-slavery conventions, these social reformers never tired of urging the view that not only Negro slavery but *all* slavery must be abolished.

Thus on May 27, 1845, at a convention of the New England Anti-Slavery Society, Robert Owen took the floor, and said that "from an early period he was opposed to Negro slavery, and also to slavery of all kinds. At home in England he had seen by far worse slavery than any he had witnessed among the colored population—all should look at the *great causes* of slavery. They could be traced to the spirit of inequality in and under all governments—all we wanted was the establishment of equal rights over all lands and countries. The black man proclaimed liberty for his color—but he stood there to contend for liberty to the white man, who was bound to the most arrant slavery of all. They were slaves, mentally and physically, to an unequal system of government, both here and in England, which crushed the laborer and the poor man everywhere down to the dust."*

In a series of articles on "The Question of Social Reform," published in the *Liberator* in 1845, Albert Brisbane, the well-known exponent of Fourier's ideas in America, speaks of "the

---

* *Liberator,* Boston, June 6, 1845.

institution of slavery" in its numerous varieties
Besides the slavery of race or color and the
slavery of capital, he speaks of foreign slavery,
home slavery, compound slavery, slavery of caste.
slavery of the soil and military slavery.   The
slavery of capital he defines as follows:

"Slavery of capital, under which man is the
dependent drudge, and the menial of the power
of money, and must sell his time, labor and talents—which is equivalent to selling himself day
by day, or by retail—to him who has the means
of buying them.   With a thick population, and
anarchical competition among the laboring classes
for work, the toiling millions are subjected, under this variety of servitude, to the most pro-
longed and oppressive drudgery, and reduced to
the most abject poverty and destitution.   This
miserable system, which wears out the souls and
bodies of the working classes enriching the few,
and leaves them and their families to starve in
sickness and old age, is only a modification of
serfdom and one degree above slavery; it sways
with iron rule the destinies of the laboring classes,
where slavery and serfdom no longer crush them
to the earth.

"If there is a reform which is imperiously demanded, it is a reform of this *servitude to capital,*
which is sinking the working classes of this
country into poverty and dependence, blotting out
their manhood, and thus destroying morally the

only population on earth which has the intelligence and the political power to effect a great and universal reform that will redeem the whole of the human family from the condition in which they are sunk. It would be a noble step, it strikes me, if the advanced guard of the Abolitionists would include in their movement a reform of the present wretched organization of labor, called the wage system. It would add to their power by interesting the producing classes in a great industrial reform including chattel slavery, and would prepare a better state for the slaves when emancipated, than that of servitude to capital, to which they now seem to be destined."*

It is surely needless to note especially the fact that Brisbane's appeal to the Abolitionists was in vain. They were unable to understand him and the aspirations of the workingmen, and to some extent probably did not want to understand.

It was at this time, in the summer of 1845, while Brisbane was publishing his series of articles, that Horace Greeley issued his celebrated definition of slavery. He had been invited to attend an anti-slavery convention. He declined the invitation and took occasion to show wherein he disagreed with the callers of the convention, his aim being to unite *all* opponents of slavery

* *Liberator,* Sept. 5, 1845.

and of *all* slavery. He raised the question: What is slavery? and answered it as follows:

"What is slavery? You will probably answer. 'The legal subjection of one human being to the will and power of another.' But this definition appears to me inaccurate on both sides—too broad, and at the same time too narrow. It is too broad, in that it includes the subjection founded in other necessities, not less stringent than those imposed by statute. We must seek some truer definition.

"I understand by slavery, that condition in which one human being exists mainly as a convenience for other human beings—in which the time, the exertions, the faculties of a part of the human family are made to subserve, not their own development, physical, intellectual and moral, but the comfort, advantage or caprices of others. In short, wherever service is rendered from one human being to another, on a footing of one-sided and not of mutual obligation—where the relation between the servant and the served is one not of affection and reciprocal good offices, but of authority, social ascendency and power over subsistence on the one hand, and of necessity, servility and degradation on the other —there, in my view, is slavery.

"You will readily understand, therefore, that, if I regard your enterprise with less absorbing interest than you do, it is not that I deem slavery a less, but a greater evil. If I am less troubled concerning the slavery prevalent in Charleston or New Orleans, it is because I see so much slavery in New York, which appears to claim my first efforts. I rejoice in believing that there is less of it in your several communities and neighbor-hoods; but that it does exist there, I am compelled to believe. In esteeming it my duty to preach reform first to my own neighbor and kindred, I would by no means attempt to censure those whose conscience prescribes a different course. Still less would I undertake to say that the slavery of the South is not more hideous in kind and degree than that which prevails at the North. The fact that it *is* more flagrant and palpable renders opposition to it comparatively easy and its speedy downfall certain. But how can I de-vote myself to a crusade against distant servitude, when I discern its essence pervading my immedi-ate community and neighborhood? nay, when I have not yet succeeded in banishing it even from my own humble household? Wherever may lie the sphere of duty of others, is not mine obviously *here?*

"Let me state what I conceive to be the essen-tial characteristics of human slavery:

"1. Wherever certain human beings devote their time and thoughts mainly to obeying and serving other human beings, and this not because they choose to do so, but because they *must,* there (I think) is slavery.

"2. Wherever human beings exist in such relations that a part, because of the position they occupy and the functions they perform, are generally considered an inferior class to those who perform other functions, or none, there (I think) is slavery.

"3. Wherever the ownership of the soil is so engrossed by a small part of the community that the far larger number are compelled to pay whatever the few may see fit to exact for the privilege of occupying and cultivating the earth, there is something very like slavery.

"4. Wherever opportunity to labor is obtained with difficulty, and is so deficient that the employing class may virtually prescribe their own terms and pay the laborer only such share as they choose of the product, there is a very strong tendency to slavery.

"5. Wherever it is deemed more reputable to live without labor than by labor, so that 'a gentleman' would be rather ashamed of his descent from a blacksmith than from an idler or mere pleasure-seeker, there is a community not very far from slavery. And—

"6. Wherever one human being deems it honorable and right to have other human beings mainly devoted to his or her convenience or comfort, and thus to live, diverting the labor of these

persons from all productive or general usefulness to his or her own special uses, while he or
she is rendering or has rendered no corresponding service to the cause of human well-being,
there exists the spirit which originated and still
sustains human slavery.

"I might multiply these illustrations indefin-
itely, but I dare not so trespass on your patience.
Rather allow me to apply the principles here
evolved in illustration of what I deem the duties
and policy of Abolitionists in reference to their
cause. And here I would advise:

"Oppose slavery in all its forms. Be at least
as careful not to *be* a slave-holder as not to *vote*
for one. Be as tenacious that your own wives,
children, hired men and women, tenants, etc.,
enjoy the blessings of rational liberty, as that the
slaves of South Carolina do. . . . ."

Whether it was that men like Owen, Brisbane,
Greeley and others influenced the leaders of the
Abolitionists, or whether these independently
came to see that it would amount to cutting off
the branch on which they were sitting if they
persisted in challenging the hostility of the labor
movement, the fact is that the attacks of Garrison and his friends on the independent organization of the working class were in the main
confined to the first beginnings of the Abolitionist movement. They soon ceased, and the old
antagonism found vent only now and again, on

special occasions. Of course, the early attempts at an independent political labor movement in New England and in New York in the thirties were doomed to failure. The crises of 1837 put an end also to the frail beginnings of trade-union organizations, so that there was little occasion for collision between the Abolitionists and the labor movement. But it seems also that the spokesmen of the former came to the conclusion that it would be in the interest of their own agitation if they left the labor organizations in peace.

Some of the Abolitionist leaders gradually even came to conceive sound views in regard to the labor question. Most noted among these was Wendell Phillips, who in later years, after the abolition of Negro slavery had been accomplished, thoroughly identified himself with the emancipatory aspirations of the workingmen. In a speech delivered in 1847 before the Anti-Slavery Society in Boston, he suggested, for instance, that people cease using the products of slave labor—in other words, that they declare a boycott against Southern goods. On this occasion he expressed himself as follows:

"In my opinion the great question of labor, when it shall come up, will be found paramount to others, and the operatives of New England, peasants of Ireland and laborers of South America, will not be lost sight of in the sympathy for the Southern slave."

A labor paper, in calling attention to these remarks, said:

"Mr. Phillips is on the high road to the principles of social reform. May he and like philan-
thropists be brought to see that slavery, war,
poverty and oppression are inseparable from the
system of civilization, the system of antagonism
of interest; that the only effectual remedy is the
introduction of a higher system of union of interest and union of industry."*

In the middle of the forties an active labor
movement sprang into being which sought to extend its activities alike over the political and the
economic field. Gatherings and labor conventions were of daily occurrence, everywhere labor
organizations were formed and labor papers
started. The organized workingmen emphasized
their sympathy for the Negro slaves of the
South, but did not fail to point out again and
again the necessity for the abolition of wage
slavery. In an appeal to the workingmen of New
England, L. W. Ryckman, president of the New
England Workingmen's Association, called on
them to "abolish *all* slavery, by connecting the
obligation to cultivate, with the right to own
the land." **

Half a year later, on January 16, 1846, a con-

---

* George E. McNeil: *The Labor Movement*. 1887. p.
113.
** *Liberator*, July 4, 1845.

vention of New England workingmen met at
Lynn, Mass., and took such unequivocal ground
against Negro slavery as to make it perfectly
clear that the special emphasis placed on the class
interests of the workingmen, the demand for the
abolition of *all* slavery, certainly did not imply
any friendship for the slaveholders of the South
and for Negro slavery. Public opinion in the
United States at that time was excited by the
impending war with Mexico for the possession
of Texas—a war, in fact, waged for the extension of Negro slavery and in the interest of the
slaveholders. A resolution was adopted at this
convention which is characteristic of the uncom-
promising sentiments entertained by the workingmen of the North, despite the opposition of the
Abolitionists to their demands. This resolution
was worded:

"Whereas, there are at the present time three
millions of our brethren and sisters groaning in
chains on the Southern plantations; and, whereas, we wish not only to be consistent, but to
secure to all others those rights and privileges
for which we are contending ourselves; therefore,

"Resolved, that while we honor and respect our
forefathers for the noble manner in which they
resisted British oppression, we, their descendants,
will never be guilty of the glaring inconsistency
of taking up arms to shoot and to stab those who

use the same means to accomplish the same objects.

"Resolved, that while we are willing to pledge ourselves to use all means in our power, consistent with our principles, to put down wars, insurrections and mobs, and to protect all men from the evils of the same, we will not take up arms to sustain the Southern slaveholders in robbing one-fifth of our countrymen of their labor.

"Resolved, that we recommend our brethren to speak out in thunder tones, both as associations and as individuals, and to let it no longer be said that Northern laborers, while they are contending for their rights, are a standing army to keep three millions of their brethren and sisters in bondage at the point of the bayonet."*

Among the labor papers which the new movement had called into life, *The Working Men's Advocate*, with George H. Evans as editor, was one of the most prominent. Later, in 1846, the paper changed its title to *Young America*, and in the main championed the demands of the Free Soilers, but for the rest remained a stanch defender of the interests of labor. In this paper the antagonism between the Abolitionists and the labor movement was pointedly revealed, and occasionally Evans did not hesitate to declare himself quite frankly against Negro emancipation, on the

---

* McNeil: *The Labor Movement.* p. 107.

ground that in his opinion the blacks would be economically in a worse position under the system of wage labor than they were under slavery.

Evans felt especially embittered over the fact that in England, where the Abolitionists had many connections and where a great outcry was made against Negro slavery, no voice was raised within the ruling classes against the frightful conditions produced by industrial development among wide sections of the English workingmen. In *Young America* he reproached particularly the English correspondents of Garrison's *Liberator* with "never having a word to say against the worse slavery of the plundered landless of England." Wendell Phillips protested against this assertion and declared the statements of Evans to be false. Evans replied in *Young America:*

"If it is betime as I most firmly believe it is, that wage slavery in its legitimate results of crowded cities, debasing servitude, rent exactions, disease, crime and prostitution, as they now appear in England and in our Northern and Eastern States, are even more destructive of life. health and happiness than chattel slavery, as it exists in our Southern States, then the efforts of those who are endeavoring to substitute wages for chattel slavery are greatly misdirected, and if they cannot be convinced of their error, they should, if possible, be prevented from making more converts to their erroneous doctrine. . . . .

". . . .As the *Liberator's* correspondents seldom, if ever, allude to the giant wrong of England, the usurpation of the soil, which makes the working classes the slaves of wages, they are probably in as blissful ignorance of any wrong in the matter as the 'young master' of a Southern plantation who believes that he was born to be waited upon by the dark skins.

"Those who, like the editor of the *Liberator*, are willing to devote themselves to the object of redressing the manifest injustice of society, cannot well afford to be divided in their forces. . . . . The National Reform measures would not merely substitute one form of slavery for another, but would replace every form of slavery by entire freedom."*

In a communication to the editor of the *Liberator* in which he thanked him for publishing Evans' reply to Phillips, William West attempted to soften its harshness. He wrote, among other things: "They [the workingmen] do not hate chattel slavery less, but they hate wage slavery more. Their rallying cry is: 'Down with all slavery, both chattel and wages.' "

But Evans had become so obsessed with the idea that wage slavery was a harder lot than the slavery of the Negro, and he was so convinced that the realization of the programme of the Na-

---

* *Liberator,* Sept. 4, 1846.

tional Reformers and of "free land" would remove all evils, that he completely lost sight of the importance of the solution of the question of Negro slavery. He had no comprehension of the fact that the solution of the question of Negro slavery was a condition precedent to the success of the labor movement. He regarded the emancipation of the workingmen from wage slavery with a certain religious fanaticism, with the result that he became embroiled in controversies not only with the Abolitionists, as against whom he was in the right, but also with the leaders and champions of the working class itself, and in these was often carried to such extremes by his religio-fanatical zeal that his hatred of the white slavery of the wage laborers came near turning into a defence of Negro slavery.

In April, 1844, there appeared in the chief organ of the English Chartists, the *Northern Star* of Leeds, published by Feargus O'Connor, a leading article entitled "Abuses of American Republicanism." As the first count in illustration of the abuse of republicanism in America we find cited here Negro slavery, concerning which O'Connor wrote:

"That damning stain upon the American escutcheon is one that has caused the republicans of Europe to weep for very shame and mortification; and the people of the United States have much to answer for at the bar of humanity for

this indecent, cruel, revolting and fiendish violation of their boasted principle—that 'All men are
born free and equal.' "

Another abuse of American republicanism
O'Connor found in the fact that the struggle of
the working classes of England, "their own kith
and kin," had excited no sympathy among the
Americans. "With a million times the difficul-
ties to contend with that the Americans had, the
English Chartists have been ridiculed and cul-
minated by a no small section of the republican
(?) press for seeking the establishment of the
very principles of the *Declaration of Independence.* But this we cease to be surprised at,
when we find the patriots of Rhode Island treated
as 'rebels' for demanding universal suffrage."

For Evans the conditions in England and the
lot of the workingmen there represented the depth
of degradation, and he consequently did not receive O'Connor's attack on America good-natur-
edly. He replied to it in an article in the *Working Men's Advocate* of June 1, 1844, in which
he said, among other things:

"The *Northern Star* does not seem to understand the difficulty of the slavery system which
British rule has entailed on this country; does
not appear to know that the *white* slave states
have no more to do with the *black* slave states
on this question than they have with England;
does not appear to see that a restoration of the

right to land would strike at the root of *all*
slavery.

"We of the North may sympathize with the
Southern slave, who is *secure* of a home and a
subsistence, such as they are, at every stage of
factory slave of England, whose toil is harder
and whose fare is more scanty than the blacks
while able to work, and who must starve or be a
prisoner in his premature old age; but, while the
same abuse is in quick operation among ourselves
from which *both* systems of slavery have sprung,
and while we 'have the axe,' shall we waste our
time in fruitless sympathy, or shall we *ply* the
instrument to the roots of the upas?"

Evans held that the solution of the question of
wage slavery contained the solution of all other
questions, consequently also of Negro slavery,
and he believed so firmly in this solution through
the realization of the free land plank of the National Reformers, which was to guarantee to
every citizen 160 acres of land, that he regarded
all other aspirations as superfluous and directed
his own efforts stubbornly toward this one end.
Notwithstanding that he compared the more secure lot of the Negro slaves to the uncertain life
of the wage workers, he was far from seeing re-
dress in the further enslavement of the latter.
He hated both forms of slavery equally, and only
set forth the dark sides of wage slavery the more
glaringly because he believed that it depended

simply on the good will of men whether or not wage slavery could be abolished. In his view men needed only to will it, in order to revolutionize, reorganize and improve society. Neither Evans, nor the social reformers of all shades, nor the workingmen in the forties knew anything about the historical and economic prerequisites for such change. This fact explains why some of them regarded the emancipation of the Negro slaves as superfluous. Why, they argued, agitate for the abolition of Negro slavery if by the same effort not only the slavery of the blacks but also the slavery of the whites, of the wage laborers, may be abolished? This reasoning, moreover, explains the zeal with which Evans attempted to convert prominent Abolitionists to his views.

One of the Abolitionists who had won great fame as a champion of his cause was Gerrit Smith of New York, a wealthy landowner and philanthropist, to whom Evans addressed an open letter with the appeal that he devote himself to the cause of the workingmen and the National Reformers. He wrote, in part:

"All I ask of you is, seeing as I trust you now do, that white as well as black slavery is wrong, that you lend your aid to prevent the further extension of the evil; to prevent any further sale of the land that is now unappropriated as private property; that you take the mote out of your own

eye, before you attempt to pluck that out of your
neighbor's. . . . .

". . . . I was formerly, like yourself, sir, a
very warm advocate of the abolition of slavery.
This was before I saw that there was *white*
slavery. Since I saw this, I have materially
changed my views as to the means of abolishing
Negro slavery. I now see, clearly, I think, that
to give the landless black the privilege of changing masters now possessed by the landless *white,*
would hardly be a benefit to him in exchange for
his surity of support in sickness and old age, although he is in a favorable climate. If the Southern form of slavery existed at the North, I should
say the black would be a great loser by such a
change."*

Smith frankly admitted that he did not understand Evans' reasoning, and declared that he had
never before heard similar opinions expressed
and that he could not accept them. Smith was
subsequently elected (1852) to the lower house
of Congress as an Abolitionist. That his views
had undergone considerable change in the meantime is evidenced by the following extract from
a speech delivered in Congress in 1854:

"The world will be much happier when land
monopoly shall cease, because manual labor will
then be so honorable, because so well-nigh uni-

Working Men's Advocate, July 4, 1844.

versal. It will be happier, too, because the wage system, with all its attendant degradation and unhappy influences, will find but little room in the new and radically changed condition of society."

The position of Evans and his friends is very neatly brought out in a series of parables which he quoted in his paper: "The poor Negro," he said, "must work for others or be flogged; the poor white man must work for others, or be starved. The poor Negro is subjected to a single master; the poor white man is subjected to many masters—to a master class. The poor Negro leads the life of a farm-horse; the poor white man, like a horse kept at a livery stable, is worked by everybody and cared for by nobody. The poor Negro has a master both in sickness and in health; the poor white man is a slave only so long as he is able to toil, and a pauper when he can toil no more."*

Only a few of the labor leaders of that period were carried to such extremes by their bitterness as was Evans, who in his work and zeal in behalf of the emancipation of the wage workers almost became a champion of Negro slavery. The mass of the organized workingmen of the Northeastern portion of the country remained hostile to Negro slavery; they were among the most enthusiastic agitators in the Abolitionist

---

* *Working Men's Advocate,* June 22, 1844.

cause. But they never failed, in the interest of their class, to emphasize the desirability of the improvement of their own lot and the necessity of the abolition of wage slavery.

The Revolution of 1848 in Europe met with a ready response in America and gave a fresh impetus to both Abolitionism and the labor move‧ment. When the news reached these shores of the insurrection of the people of Paris in February, 1848, a whole series of labor meetings, and especially trade-union meetings, was called to pass resolutions conveying to the people of Paris the felicitation of the American working class. On May 9th a mass meeting of the workingmen of Boston was called in Faneuil Hall for the purpose of expressing their sympathies with the workingmen of Europe and of discussing the state of labor movement in America. Albert T. Wright was the chairman of the meeting. Some of the resolutions passed congratulated the working people of France and the Provisional Government in Paris and expressed the sympathy of the workingmen of Boston for the Chartists in England and the Repealers in Ireland. A further resolution passed by the meeting was as follows:

"While we rejoice in the organization of free institutions in the old world, we are not indifferent to their support at home, and we regret the despotic attitude of the slave power at the South, and the domineering ascendency of the monied oligarchy in the North as equally hostile to the interests of labor, and incompatible with the preservation of popular rights.

"Resolved, that if we would procure the passage of just and efficient laws to protect labor, and raise it from its present degrading dependence on wealth, we must purge the halls of legislation of the hirelings who basely pander to the interests of capital, and to accomplish this result we recommend for the laboring classes to try for once the experiment of trusting the management of their political affairs to men of their own class, who know their interests and have a fellow-feeling in supporting them."*

As we see, the industrial workingmen still clung to the idea that it was not alone the Southern oligarchy of slaveholders, but also the money power of the North, that had to be combated—a view which survived into the fifties, but which thereafter was less emphasized, presumably because the social reformers of different tendencies who had stirred the working masses by the cry of wage slavery gradually began to disappear from the scene.

As the movement against Negro slavery gained in momentum, the conviction that the slavery of the blacks was doomed naturally took firmer hold also of the working class. We note here the fact,

---

* McNeil. p. 115.

easily enough to be explained, that the working classes of the purely industrial centers, especially of New England, took a more decided stand against Negro slavery than those of the large cities like Boston and New York, where Democratic influences were active in behalf of the slaveholders and where, through commerce, various economical considerations tended to dispose the workingmen in favor of Negro slavery.

2. The German Workingmen in America and Slavery.

In the forties and fifties the immigrant German workingmen played an important part in the United States, especially in New York and its vicinity. Entire trades were in their hands, and from the start they took an active part in the labor movement. Indeed, they were the pioneers of the modern radical wing.

In their travels through Switzerland, France and England, German workingmen of that period were powerfully influenced by the secret Communist organizations which had everywhere sprung into life. Members of the *Bund der Gerechten,* of the *Kommunisten-Bund,* of Weitling's workingmen's leagues, of the workingmen's societies for self-culture in Switzerland, Paris and London, came flocking to the United States and made converts to their views. In the middle of the forties, on the initiative of a certain Hermann Kriege, there was formed a branch society of the *Bund der Gerechten,* from which sprang a German branch, *Jung Amerika,* which took up and championed the demands of the American land reformers.

By the end of the forties the German labor organizations had already attained to great power and influence. Often, on Sunday afternoons, in the public parks, one could hear addresses in the German language propagating Communist ideas, though not very clearly defined. The Communist propaganda was, moreover, supported by weekly papers in New York, Philadelphia and St. Louis; and when, in 1848, the overthrow of the Revolution drove tens of thousands of revolutionary Germans to America, the number of these Socialist Communist papers was very largely increased.

We have seen that the workingmen of New England early defined their position in regard to Negro slavery. They condemned it, but at the same time always emphasized the necessity of abolishing wage labor, which they described, much to the chagrin of the Abolitionists, as "white slavery."

This position, which was assigned to the workingmen by their dawning class consciousness, we find also taken by the German workingmen of this country, especially those of New York, only with greater intensity, presumably because they had developed a profounder understanding of the aims and ends of the labor movement. The consciousness of the necessity of the struggle to achieve their own emancipation carried these workingmen to such extremes as to dispose certain sections of them, under demagogic influence, even in favor of slavery. They failed to perceive the historical necessity of the abolition of Negro slavery as a condition precedent to the improvement of their own lot.

In an article in a New York labor paper, entitled "Our Position on the Issues of the Day," in 1846, Hermann Kriege declared with special reference to the slavery question:

"That we see in the slavery question a property question which cannot be settled by itself alone. That we should declare ourselves in favor of the Abolitionist movement if it were our intention to throw the Republic into a state of anarchy, to extend the competition of 'free workingmen' beyond all measure, and to depress labor itself to the last extremity. That we could not improve the lot of our 'black brothers' by abolition under the conditions prevailing in modern society, but make infinitely worse the lot of our 'white brothers.' That we believe in the peaceable development of society in the United States and do not, therefore, here at least see our only hope in a condition of the extremest degradation. That we feel constrained, therefore, to oppose Abolition with all

our might, despite all the importunities of sentimental philistines and despite all the poetical effu-
sions of liberty-intoxicated ladies."

Wilhelm Weitling, the German Communist
who came to America in 1847 and started a lively
agitation among the German workingmen, also
had only disdain for the Abolitionists, and gave
only scant attention to the question of slavery,
which at the time of his public career was beginning to crowd out all other questions. He indeed
never forgot himself so far as to vent his spleen
against the Abolitionists in the silly fashion of
Kriege (who had evidently been influenced by
George H. Evans) or to openly side with the
slaveholder. But we search in vain the columns
of the labor paper which Weitling published in
New York during the fifties, or his other public
utterances, for an explicit condemnation of
slavery—for an allusion to the fact that in its
own interest the working class of the North was
bound to combat with all its might the superan-
nuated system of production by slaves.

The first German labor convention which met
at Philadelphia in 1850 under the lead of Weitling passed a series of resolutions of a political
nature, but not a word did they contain against
slavery, not a plank with any reference to the one
question which even at that time was beginning
to inflame the public mind, and in regard to which,
as we have shown, the native American working-

men of the industrial sections of the North had expressed themselves in no uncertain tone.

In treating of Kriege and Weitling we must note the fact that both joined the Democratic party. The former did so from demagogism, the latter from conviction, a conviction which grew out of the circumstances that the opposition party, the Whigs of that time, contained a large sprinkling of elements hostile to labor, and especially out of the further circumstance that the elements hostile to foreigners, the Know-nothings, who rose to the surface in the beginning and the middle of the fifties, exercised great influence in the councils of this party. It must be ascribed to this circumstance that large numbers of immigrant Germans joined the Democrats, the opponents of the Whigs. But the Democrats stood also for the maintenance and extension of Negro slavery, and their German following—including the German workingmen—in their ignorance of American conditions and their confusion in economic matters, joined in the Democratic battle cry in behalf of slavery.

Little was known, moreover, in these labor circles concerning the economic significance of the slavery question. They betrayed scant intelligence in dealing with it, and in so far as they discussed it at all they did so from the point of view of the political party which they favored and from the point of view of the sentiments

which governed them.   And the radical and
progressive workingmen, like their English-
speaking brothers in New England and New
York, scented in the agitation of the slavery
question a peril to their own agitation, the aim
of which was the emancipation of the white
workingmen, the wage workers.   In their opinion, participation in the anti-slavery movement
diverted the attention of the German workingmen from their own struggles and caused them,
in their interest in what was considered a matter of secondary importance, to forget that which
was of prime importance, their own emancipation.

Under the controlling influence of Joseph
Weydemeyer, a friend of Karl Marx, the *Arbeiterbund* (the Workingmen's League) was
founded in March, 1853.   The *Arbeiterbund,*
which was distinguished from the labor organizations founded by Weitling and Kriege by a
greater definiteness of aim, originally also gave
little heed if any to the question of slavery, and
its platform contained no plank referring to it.
But when the question became a burning one the
Arbeiterbund defined its position, and as on the
labor question so now on the slavery question it
was well advised by its counsellors.   In a mass
meeting called by the *Arbeiterbund* in New York
on March 1, 1854, the following resolution was
adopted:

"Whereas, capitalism and land speculation have again been favored at the expense of the mass of the people by the passage of the Nebraska Bill;

"Whereas, this bill withdraws from or makes unavailable in a future homestead bill vast tracts of territory;

"Whereas, this bill authorizes the further extension of slavery, but we have, do now, and shall continue to protest most emphatically against both white and black slavery;

"Whereas, finally, we desire to consider and shape our own welfare, free from the dictation of lawmakers, wire-pullers and the hireling masses;

"Therefore, be it resolved that we solemnly protest against this bill and brand as a traitor against the people and their welfare every one who shall lend it his support."

This emphatic declaration against the Kansas-Nebraska Bill is explained by the fact that it actually opened the entire West to slavery. The *New York Staats-Zeitung,* Democratic and pro-slavery, on the occasion of the introduction of this bill counselled people everywhere to abstain from all agitation against the extension of slavery, and thereby incurred the lively opposition of the entire liberal German population of New York. The passage in the above resolution of the *Arbeiterbund* referring to traitors against the people and their welfare presumably was aimed at the newspaper.

With the advance and cumulative intensity of the Abolitionist agitation, and with the culminating political antagonisms between the North and the South, the German workingmen gathered in the *Arbeiterbund*, gave increased attention to the question of slavery, and a large number of them, the clearer headed, ranged themselves uncompromisingly on the side of the Abolitionists. Individual organizations, such as the Communist Club, contributed liberally toward spreading the light on this question, and they were so downright in their opposition to the slaveholders as to call any of their members promptly to account who fell under the slightest suspicion of sympathizing with the South. A number of the gymnastic societies—the *Socialen Turn-Vereine*—also strongly opposed slavery and embodied in their platforms and resolutions planks demanding its abolition.

Slavery did not, however, so engross the attention of the organizations of German workingmen at this period as to crowd out all other questions. When in December, 1857, the *Arbeiterbund* reorganized, and a new platform was adopted, slavery was not even mentioned in it. The question which at that time was stirring and agitating other people everywhere was simply ignored. And when in April, 1858, the *Soziale*

Republic appeared as the organ of the *Arbeiter-bund,* its expressions on slavery were very luke-warm. The management of the paper held that for the time being the institution of Negro slavery was still firmly rooted in America. We find this statement in the first issue of the paper, April 24, 1858: "The question of the present moment is not the abolition of slavery, but the prevention of its further extension"; and again: "At this moment the question of the abolition of slavery is still remote."

Although the policy of the *Soziale Republik* here indicated betrays small political sagacity, it shows no open hostility to the abolition of slavery. The editors of the paper merely believed slavery to be more firmly rooted than it really was.

But matters were different with another division of the German workingmen's organizations in New York. This division was not very powerful and was of but short duration. It had seceded from the *Arbeiterbund* in 1857, and was under the lead of a certain W. Banque, who published in New York a German labor paper entitled *Der Arbeiter.* It had further framed a platform, with these planks:

"Abolition of slavery in two steps: (a) Abolition of the slave trade; (b) introduction of the apprenticeship system; opening up of the continents, civilizing Africa and South America through emancipated slaves; transplantation of the plantation and apprentice system to Mexico and Central America under the authority of the United States."

In reality these planks were not directed against slavery at all. But popular sentiment against the institution of slavery had become so powerful that in the North no one dared openly oppose it any longer, and could do so only indirectly and by qualified expression. As against the plank of the Abolitionists demanding the immediate and complete abolition of slavery, which was becoming very popular, this division of the *Arbeiterbund* and the editor of *Der Arbeiter* demanded merely cessation of the slave trade and slave culture, and for the rest left slavery itself untouched. In a series of articles the editor dissuaded German workingmen from joining in the boycott declared by the Abolitionists against Southern products. They were told that they could not afford to do it because they could not live without cotton, the chief staple of the Southern plantations. There was also an attempt at a vindication of the Southern slaveholders, by extolling their humanitarian aspirations. It was stated that many slaves were set free by them, provided with money, and thus enabled to settle in the free States; also that some were sent to the west coast of Africa, to Liberia, to live in freedom there. In regard to the agitation for the abolition of slavery the editor wrote: "In so far as the agitation aims at the destruction of the *institution as a whole,* threatening at the same time to destroy the Southern plantations, it fails of its full effect, because men even of the Middle and Northern States, for the best of reasons, must declare in favor of the unconditional retention of the plantation."

Banque advocated the liberation of Negroes by purchase and the substitution in their place of "free Chinamen," of whom there was an excess and who would supply cheap labor. "The freedom of the Negroes may be effected by means of the money gained from the sale of the public lands."

By the so-called "apprenticeship system," of which mention is made in the platform of this division of the *Arbeiterbund,* the Southern Coast States, whose staples were cotton, rice and sugar, were to be empowered to exchange those of their black workingmen who "were touched by civilization and had become stubborn, intractable and insurrectionary," for fresh Africans to be imported on time and under contract. The warships of the United States were to convey the freed workers to Africa, where they were to put to use the instruction gained in America, plow, sow and reap, and exchange the products of the new soil against our "labor of superior enjoyment." It was further demanded that this "apprenticeship system" should be extended also over Mexico and Central America "under the authority of the United States." In other words, the aim was, by means of the "apprenticeship system," to conquer for the United States, but mainly in the interest of the slaveholding element, the Spanish-American countries lying south of the Union. The "apprenticeship system," indeed, meant nothing else than an extension of the slave trade.

It was charged by the opponents of the editor of *Der Arbeiter* within the *Arbeiterbund,* that is, by the German workingmen opposed to slavery, that Banque was subsidized by the party of the slaveholders and that a daily newspaper subsequently founded by him was also supported by them. Banque's whole conduct in regard to slavery lends probability to this accusation, although it need not be assumed that he was directly influenced by the slaveholders, but rather by the Democratic party of the North. He could, however, explain and in a measure justify his conduct by pointing to the original platform of the *Arbeiterbund,* which was silent in regard to slavery, and consequently left him free to treat the question in accordance with his own judgment.

The editor of *Der Arbeiter* was probably the last of the spokesmen of the German workingmen of New York who openly advocated Negro slavery—the last and, with the exception of the eccentric Kriege, the only one.   Many of the others failed to appreciate the full significance of the solution of this question, but none ever sank so low as to undertake an open defence of the institution and of the Southern slaveholders.

After the *Arbeiterbund* had cast off Banque, mainly on account of his friendly attitude toward slavery, a somewhat firmer tone in regard to this issue began to prevail in the organ of the main body, the *Soziale Republik*.   Only gradually, of course; for as late as November, 1858, it warned its readers against overlooking, in the conflict between liberty and slavery, "the other burning issues of the day."   And again: "Not only years, but more likely decades, will pass before this great conflict is decided."   That these pessimistic expressions of the *Soziale Republik* reflected the dominant sentiment of the *Arbeiterbund* is made plain by the conduct of the society's first convention in 1859.   This convention adopted the following resolution in regard to slavery.

"We condemn all slavery, in whatever form it may appear, and we pledge ourselves to combat it with all the means at our disposal.   We especially demand the immediate repeal of the Fugitive Slave Law."

In principle the wording of this resolution was entirely correct.   But there are times when placing the emphasis on the purely theoretical posi-

tion amounts to an impairment of this position.
This was the case here, where the practical demand of the immediate abolition of slavery would
at the same time have meant a more emphatic
avowal of the theoretical position of the German
workingmen.

But the rapid succession of events and the de-
fiant attitude of the slave barons presently led
to a profounder insight among the men of the
Soziale Republik and the *Arbeiterbund*.   They
roused themselves and offered a more stubborn
opposition to slavery, without, however, attain-
ing to a full theoretical comprehension of the
question.   It was especially in the last months
of its existence, under the editorship of J. Rödel,
that the *Soziale Republik* uncompromisingly
championed the abolition of slavery and urged
the cause in the circles of the German workingmen.   And when the crisis came, and force assumed the direction of things, a large portion of
the German workingmen and their spokesmen
obeyed the call to arms, in order to fight on the
side of the North, and against the slaveholders
and their armies.   We mention among the better
known: Gustav Struve, Jos. Weydemeyer, F.
Annecke, August Willich, Rudolph Rosa, Fritz
Jacobi, Dr. Beust.   There were still others who
so distinguished themselves in the skirmishes and
battles of the Civil War as to rise to high rank,

while many others gave their lives for the emancipation of the Negro.

3. THE WHITE WORKINGMEN OF THE SOUTH.

The population of the Southern States previous to the Civil War was composed not only of slaveholders and slaves, but there was an intermediate stratum which, in the controversies of that period, was not mentioned as often as the former, though it was by far the more numerous. This stratum consisted of the white non-slaveholders.

There was in the South a number of Christian sects which, from religious motives, kept no slaves and whose adherents either did their own work themselves or had it done for them by paid free wage workers. The number of free white agricultural laborers in the South alone amounted to a million in 1850. There was also a considerable number of independent farmers, who for one reason or another, declined to have anything to do with slavery. Added to these were the merchants, clerks, teachers and men of similar callings. But the bulk of these non-slaveholders among the white population of the South, outside of the agricultural laborers, was formed by mechanics, artisans, skilled workers and the numerous laborers who gained their livelihood in the most various enterprises and callings.

Although, as we have said, but small mention was made of the white non-slaveholders of the

South, they formed the most numerous part of the population there. Of a total population of 9,500,000 in the Southern States in 1850 the actual slaveholders with their families did not constitute quite 2,000,000, and these claimed 3,500,-000 slaves as their own. The remainder of the population, about 4,250,000, was composed of the white non-slaveholders, the great majority of whom were either proletarians or the "dangerous class," the scum of society.

The slaveholders themselves as a whole did not form a homogeneous stratum. At the apex of the pyramid of Southern society were the large landed proprietors, according to the census of 1850 about 8,000 in number, each with fifty or more slaves. They were followed by the stratum, about 165,000 persons in 1850, who owned from five to fifty Negro slaves. After these came the lowest stratum of the slaveholders, owning from one to four slaves each. In 1850 there were in the South 68,820 persons who owned one slave each, while 105,683 called two, three and four Negroes their own. Altogether, consequently, 174,503 persons belonged to this lowest order of the slaveholders, who were not rich enough to have slaves exclusively working for them, but who were obliged to do part of their work themselves.*

---

* Denton J. Snider: *The American Ten Years' War.* pp. 291-92.

It was the uppermost stratum, numbering 8,000 persons, who exercised political domination in the South and who determined the whole course of Southern social life. In 1850 there were only two persons among the slaveholders who owned more than 1,000 slaves. Nine owned from 500 to 1,000, fifty-six from 300 to 500, and 187 claimed as their property from 200 to 300 Negroes. These few persons constituted the apex of the uppermost stratum of the oligarchy, whose will was law in the South. Although the smaller slaveholders were connected with the ruling oligarchy of the upper 8,000 by the system of slavery, there was frequent dissatisfaction among them with the ruling policy, in consequence of conflicting interests. But notwithstanding their numerical inferiority, the large landed proprietors were in complete control of the political institutions of the country. Their sway was absolute in the Legislatures. They systematically saw to it that the poor white population should receive no public school education and deliberately kept it in the densest ignorance. They acted indeed as if these poor whites were not in existence at all. "The non-slaveholding whites of the South," observed a certain George M. Weston, "being not less than seven-tenths of the whole number of whites, would seem to be entitled to some inquiry into their actual condition. But, for twenty years, I do not recollect ever to have seen or heard these non-slaveholding whites referred to by the Southern 'gentlemen' as constituting any part of what they call 'the South.' "

The terrible ignorance of the poor whites in the South made it impossible for them to come to an understanding of their true interests, which would have ranged them in direct opposition to the landlords and slaveholders. On the lowest plane of social culture were those among them who in the immediate neighborhood of large plantations occupied impoverished and abandoned rural holdings, and who gained their meagre subsistence by hunting and fishing, by forbidden trading with Negroes, and by all kinds of dirty service for the slaveowners. They were ever the most willing tools in the hands of the Southern oligarchy, they hunted its slaves, and during the Civil War fought its battles despite the fact that this oligarchy had sinned against the ignorant whites of the South still more even than against the Negro slaves.

An American historian, speaking of the attitude maintained by the large slaveholders as against the poor whites of their States, observes:

"How is the society of which they are members fulfilling its responsibility toward them? The record is universally admitted to be bad, in fact, it is the worst count in the indictment against the Southern oligarchy, worse than the count against

them on the subject of black slavery, though this
must be regarded as the first cause of the evil."*

The fact is that the ruling slaveholders were
under the necessity of keeping the mass of the
population, including the poor whites, in ignorance and of denying them all schooling. Only
25 per cent. of the latter could read and write.
The education of these masses would have en-
dangered the dominion, would have threatened
the existence, of the slaveholders as the ruling
class. In the United States Senate the statement
was made in 1858 that "200,000 men with white
skin in South Carolina are now degraded and
despised by 30,000 slaveholders."

The ignorance, and in its wake the crimes and
the poverty of the "white trash," as the poor
whites were called by their brothers who were in
the possession of wealth and power, became so
alarming that even members of the ruling class
itself petitioned for their relief.

"In December, 1855, Governor Adams of
South Carolina urges almost frantically: 'Make
at least this effort'—the appointment of a State
Superintendent of Education—'and if the poor
of the land are hopelessly doomed to ignorance,
poverty and crime'—which he seemed to think,
'you will at least feel conscious of having done

* Snider. p. 306.

your duty, and the public anxiety on the subject will be quieted.' "*

This contrast between the rich landlords and the "white trash" had always existed. "The people of Carolina consist of two classes, the rich and the poor," as already General Marion of Revolutionary War fame had observed. "The poor in general are very poor, since they are not employed by the rich who do not need them, having slaves to work for them. Thus deprived of the support of the rich, they remain poor and oppressed. They rarely have any money, and the little that comes their way they spend for brandy to cheer their spirits; not for newspapers and books to instruct their minds."

As then, so now; as at the time of the Revolutionary War, so at the time of the Civil War; as in the Carolinas, so in the other slave states. A born Southerner who had lived a number of years in South Carolina and who had travelled extensively through Latin America, placed the poor whites of the States named even below the Spanish-Indian halfbreeds, known as *Pintos,* and declared that he had never found the latter in their most abandoned state so degraded, so feeble, so indolent and so bereft of all purpose in life as the former.

Besides the ignorance of the poor whites, the

---

* Olmstead: *Seabord Slave States.* pp. 505-6. Snider. p. 307.

slaveholders had still another support of their dominion in the social bias of all Southern whites
against the Negroes, a bias which the ruling class
did not fail carefully to cultivate. A "nigger,"
even in the eyes of the poor whites, was not a
human being, and to be placed on an equality
with one was an affront that could not be ex-
piated promptly enough in blood. This bias was
reinforced by a certain economic antagonism in
such a way that the ruling oligarchy could avail
itself of it as a lever for the maintenance and
continuation of its dominion. It was enough for
the large landed proprietors to tell the poor whites
that it was the aim of the North to place the
Negroes on an equality with the whites, to range
this entire ignorant stratum of the population,
most of whom could neither read nor write,
against the North. In explanation of the hatred
which the poor whites of the South harbored
against the Negroes, we may point to the class
antagonisms which developed between free and
unfree labor which furnished the material foundation of this hatred.

Slave labor did not merely degrade the dignity
of labor, including the labor of the free workingman, it did not merely make labor contemptible, it also depressed the wages of free workingmen, lowered their standard of life and offered the labor of the white workingmen such
sharp competition that they could not meet it.

This fact was frankly conceded by representatives of the ruling class in the South, as when Governor Cannon of Delaware stated: "Slave labor is uncompensated, white labor is compensated; when the two are brought into competition, white labor is crowded out. If capital owns its labor, the avenues to honest livelihood are forever closed to the white."

The slaveowner with his slave labor was a competitor of the free workingman. Originally the slaves were employed only on the plantations and as domestic servants. But later they were instructed in certain trades, they became mechanics, especially blacksmiths, carpenters and wagon-makers, and by displacing the white mechanics they became of especial value to their masters. Gradually the slaveholders even negotiated for the performance of mechanics' work under contract, setting their slaves to do it.

Olmsted relates that at Austin, the capital of Texas, the German mechanics complained that when labor for building the State capitol was given out, many of them came with offers, but were underbid by the owners of the slave-mechanics. But when the free mechanics had left town, in search of employment elsewhere, the slaveowners threw up their contracts, and, having no longer any opposition, obtained new contracts at advanced prices.

Charles Nordhoff states that he was told by a

wealthy Alabaman, in 1860, that the planters in
his region were determined to discontinue altogether the employment of free mechanics. "On
my own place," he said, "I have slave carpenters,
slave blacksmiths, and slave wheelwrights, and
thus I am independent of free mechanics." And
a certain Alfred E. Mathews remarks: "I have
seen free white mechanics obliged to stand aside
while their families were suffering for the necessaries of life, when the slave mechanics, owned
by rich and influential men, could get plenty of
work; and I have heard these same white mechanics breathe the most bitter curses against the
institution of slavery and the slave aristocracy."*

As soon as his interests came into play the
slaveholder put his despised "niggers" even above
the free white workingmen. A planter of Virginia employed a gang of Irishmen in draining
some land. And why did he use free labor for
this kind of unskilled work, which could have
been performed perhaps cheaper by his slaves?
"It's dangerous work, it's unwholesome, being
malarious ditches," he said, "and a negroe's life
is too valuable to be risked at it. If a negro dies,
it is a considerable loss, you know." . . . . "Slaves
are, on the southwestern steamboats, employed to
do the lightest and least dangerous labor; but
Irish and German free workingmen are employed

---

* Charles Nordhoff: *America for Free Workingmen.*
1865, p. 8.

to perform the exhausting and dangerous work."†

The development of industry in the South also furnished an occasion to the slaveowners for employing their slaves in competition with the white workingmen. As early as the fifties the beginning had been made with the erection of factories in which slaves only were employed as operatives. The wages of the white working-men, so far as they were employed, were terribly depressed in consequence of the competition of slave labor in the respective branches. While in the cotton mills of Lowell, Mass., in 1852, working men received 80 cents each per day and women 2.00 per week, the wages of free workingmen in Tennessee in the same line amounted to barely 50 cents each per day and of women $1.25 per week.

Even at these starvation wages free labor was underbid by the slaveholders. Their control of the labor market was absolute, since in any case they could produce more cheaply than free workingmen. "It matters nothing to him" [the slave-holder], says Nordhoff, "how low others can produce the article; he can produce it lower still, so long as it is the best use he can make of his labor, and as long as that labor is worth keeping A free white mechanic is at the mercy of his

---

† Nordhoff, pp. 7-8.

neighbor, the capitalist, in a slave state, because, if the capitalist does not like his price, he can go and buy a carpenter and sell him again when the work is done."

But despite the best intentions of the slave-holders, the purely industrial employment of slaves made small progress. An industrial population must first be educated and developed. But everything smacking of popular education, as already observed, was intensely offensive to the South, even the education necessary for making a good factory operative. The greatest dependence of the masses presupposes the greatest helplessness of the individuals composing them. The Southern slaveholders were as well aware of this as was the Catholic Church, which reared its authority on the same fact. It was therefore in the interest of the slaveholders to maintain their chattels in darkest ignorance, no matter how much the latter's usefulness might suffer in other ways.

There was another factor to cross the calculations of the slaveholders. Modern industry gives to workingmen a character of its own which is incompatible with slavery as it had developed in the South. Even the Negroes who were employed at industrial pursuits were touched by the spirit which transforms submissive and patient agricultural slaves into revolutionary proletarians. That great conspiracy of slaves which

spread dismay over the entire South shortly before the outbreak of the Civil War had its origin
not on the plantations, but in the Cumberland
Iron Works of Tennessee, the largest industrial
enterprise carried on with slave labor in the
South. This conspiracy gave the slaveholders a
sense of the danger with which modern industry
was threatening them.

Nevertheless, the mere attempts to organize
industry on the basis of slave labor proved an
injury to the Southern free workingmen, principally through the powerful pressure which was
thereby exerted on their wages and their standard
of life.   And that the modern, the industrial
workingmen were necessarily hostile to slavery
was instinctively felt by the slaveholders, who
promptly reciprocated this hostility with their
own profoundest hatred.   The *Standard,* an
organ of the slaveholders in Charleston, declared
in 1855:

"A large portion of the mechanical force that
migrate to the South are a curse instead of a
blessing; they are generally a worthless, unprincipled class, enemies to our peculiar institution
[slavery] and formidable barriers to the success
of our native mechanics [slaves]."

The merchants and other middle-class men
who came from the North to the Southern States
were, according to the same paper, "better qualified to become constituents of our institution

than a certain class of our native born, who from
want of capacity are perfect drones in society,
continually carping about slave competition.
The mechanics, the most of them, are pests to
society, dangerous among the slave population,
and ever ready to form combinations against the
interests of the slaveholders."

Evidently the slaveholders saw in the mechanics, the socially soundest element among the
white non-slaveholders, their natural enemy.
They took good care not to invest this enemy
with political weapons by means of which he
might imperil their own dominion. The free
white laborer in South Carolina, for instance,
could vote, but not for one of his own class;
only a slave-owner could serve in the Legislature,
only a slave-owner could be governor; and the
Legislature, composed exclusively of slave-own-
ers, appointed the judges, the magistrates, the
senators and the electors for President. And as
in South Carolina, so approximately in the other
States of the South.

Thus we see that while the free white workingmen apparently participated in the business
of the State, they were nevertheless practically
shorn of all political influence by the crafty system of the slaveholders. Although there existed
a certain class hatred against the slaveholding
obligarchy, and although the non-slaveholders
constituted the majority of the white population,

it was impossible to unite them in an organized
and general opposition against the ruling class.
Their economic interests would have forced them
into a union with the black slave population if
it had not been prevented by racial antagonism.
But also for other reasons this stratum of society lacked that homogeneous character which
might have led to the formation of an independent class with independent and conscious aims.
Racial antagonism made of the non-slaveholders
enemies of the Negro; class antagonism made
of them, in so far as they were wage workers,
enemies of Negro slavery. The terrible ignorance in which they were artificially kept made it
impossible for their class interests to transform
them into avowed opponents of the slaveholders.
In consequence of their lack of insight and their
race prejudice, they despised the Negro and failed
to see that the slaveholder was the real enemy of
their class. As Nordhoff says:

"Is it strange that the ignorant, neglected, despised free white workingman of the slave States
hates the slave? He feels that the slave injures
him in every possible way; the slave robs him
of work, the slave deprives him of bread and
clothing for his children; the slave gets the easiest
tasks, the free laborer the hardest and most dangerous; the slave steps before him whenever he
looks for a job, and has the preference everywhere, because he is the tool of a capitalist whose

influence and wealth enable him to grasp for his own benefit whatever might be of advantage to the free mechanic or laborer."

Thus the white workingman of the South *saw* things through the spectacles of his race prejudice, while his class interest should have told him that not the slaves, but the slaveholders were his enemies. Partly indeed he felt this to be so, and that recognition made of him an enemy of slavery. It even aroused him to a certain resistance, manifested in two ways, passive and active—in a very considerable emigration from the slave States on the one hand, and on the other in the attempts to improve his lot by means of petition, organization and the press.

There was for years a continuous stream of emigrants from the slave States of the South to the Northern and the Middle Western States, and it was of course exclusively non-slaveholders who fed this stream. According to the census of 1860, 399,700 Virginians were living beyond the boundaries of their native State. From Tennessee 344,765 persons had emigrated; from North Carolina, 272,606; from Maryland, 137,258; from Delaware, 32,493; from Kentucky, 331,904. It is of course true that not all of these emigrants sought refuge in the free States. But it is also true that the majority of them had gone to the Middle West, where free land held out the promise to them of a life as farmers and where there was no competition of Negroes depressing the wages of mechanics to the lowest level. The historian Snider is of the opinion that the Southern slave States sent as many settlers to the West as did the Northeastern States. And it was the social system based on slavery which drove those large numbers of emigrants out of the South.

In a certain sense this emigration from the Southern States was a blessing to the ruling oligarchy there. It diverted the rising discontent of the non-slaveholders, with its accompanying unrest, and took from the scene of action the ablest and most energetic portion who might have served as leaders of their class.* The "white trash," the non-resisting, ignorant, enfeebled and degraded element of the poor whites, remained behind, incapable of any opposition against the ruling class.

Certain traces of a spirit of self-assertion— and this leads us to the second form of resistance of the poor whites of the South—had manifested themselves among this stratum of the population for several decades. As early as 1831 white mechanics had petitioned the Legislature of Virginia to abolish the competition of slave mechanics. In 1853 the free mechanics called a meeting at Concord, N. C., in which they voiced the

---

* Snider, p. 311.

complaint that "wealthy owners of slave mechanics were in the habit of underbidding them in contracts." The free mechanic who had inaugurated and directed this movement of the white non-slaveholders was driven from the place by the ruling class.

Of greater importance than these examples of a feeble opposition of the white non-slaveholding element against the ruling oligarchy is the following:

In 1860, that is, shortly before the outbreak of the Civil War, a man named Robert C. Tharin, of Alabama, undertook to inaugurate a general movement among the white non-slaveholders of his State for the protection of their interests against the ruling class. He endeavored to set up a newspaper called the *Non-Slaveholder,* to urge the passage of a law forbidding the employment of slaves except in agricultural labor and as servants. "He thus sought to protect the free mechanics and secure them employment. For this Mr. Tharin was summarily driven from the State."*

In a controversy with a representative of the slaveholders, who opposed his aspirations, Mr. Tharin wrote:

"He had seen the rich man's negro 'come in contact' with the poor white blacksmith, the poor

---

* Nordhoff, pp. 5 and 6.

white bricklayer, carpenter, wheelwright and
agriculturist. He had seen the preference in-
variably given to the rich man's negro in all such
pursuits and trades; like me, *he* had heard the
complaints of the poor white mechanic of the
South against the very negro equality the rich
planters were rapidly bringing about. These
things he had heard and seen in Charleston, New
Orleans, Mobile, Montgomery, and Wetumpka.

"Have not the planters for years condemned
every mechanic in the South to negro equality? I
never envied the planters of Wetumpka, or, indeed, of any part of the South. My dislike to
them arose from their contemptible meanness,
their utter disregard of decency, their supercil-
ious arrogance and their daily usurpations of
power and privileges at variance with my right
and the rights of my class."*

Such language the slaveholders could not toler-
ate at a time when they were already beginning
to prepare for the war in which the very element,
the poor whites of their States whom Tharin was
summoning to a defence of their own interests,
was to furnish the soldiers who were to fight the
battles of the South against the North. Tharin's
expulsion from his native State was consequently
foredoomed. An independent movement of the
white non-slaveholders just at that moment

---

* Nordhoff, p. 6.

would have nipped in the bud the secession of the slaveholders.

It is plain that the majority of the white population of the South had no interest in the preservation of slavery. The workingmen and mechanics of this stratum of the population hated slavery because it was the cause of their own miserable social condition, because it depressed their standard of life to the level of the Negro slaves, and brought about that "equality with the Negroes" which the slaveholders had menacingly represented to them as the aim of the North. But the hatred of these white workingmen of the South was neutralized in its effect by the prejudice and race hatred which they entertained for their black class comrades, the Negroes. When hostilities between the North and the South began, the slaveholders organized these poor whites into armies and compelled the non-slaveholders and enemies of slavery to be shot to pieces and made into cripples on the battlefields for the preservation of slavery. For during the years of the war military service offered the easiest and often the only way for securing the means of subsistence; the grand ideas which ostensibly actuate soldiers have in reality ever received but scant consideration at their hands.

4. THE WORKINGMEN OF ENGLAND AND NEGRO SLAVERY.

Almost simultaneously with the rise of the Abolitionist movement in the United States, anti-slavery societies were formed in England which entered into communication with the American movement and often joined hands with it for common work. At the very time when the English middle classes were preparing to subject their own workers to the worst conceivable industrial slavery—one needs but recall the conditions prevailing among the factory population of England in the thirties and forties—a portion of these ruling classes began to preach in favor of the abolition of slavery.

The workingmen of England had ranged themselves against slavery from the start. But like their class comrades in the United States they could not overlook the hypocrisy of the ruling classes in condemning Negro slavery abroad and opposing with all their might any limitation of white slavery at home. With the contemporary English and German labor press of the United States, the labor press of Great Britain also denounced this hypocrisy. Everywhere their awakening class consciousness led workingmen to realize that while the abolition of Negro slavery was desirable, they must not forget their own slavery, wage slavery.

Bronterre O'Brien represented their position in

a specially striking manner in the radical labor papers in the thirties, in the *Poor Man's Guardian,* in *The Destructive* and others. Among other things he wrote:

"When one listens to an Abolitionist one might think that outside of the blacks there was no slave under British rule. . . . . If these scoundrels entertained a sincere hatred against slavery they would begin by abolishing it at home. . . . . He who sallies forth on a philanthropic mission in Jamaica when he needs only to go to Spitalfields (a poor section in London) to find more misery than he will be able to abolish, is either a thick-headed fool or a heartless fraud. How is it that we never hear the Buxtons or the Wilberforces complain about slavery here at home? Listen, Buxton, and we will tell you: it is because you know, you smooth-tongued rogue, that English slavery is indispensable for 'our highly civilized state.' That is the reason, Buxton! The slavery of millions is the foundation of our cannibalistic civilization. Your cannibalistic institutions are reared on this foundation—just because the millions are slaves, you and your kidney prosper so splendidly. You lose nothing by freeing the Negroes; but you would lose a great deal if you would free Englishmen."

And O'Brien explains the last statement thus:

"In the one case (that is, in England) the master employs and supports his slave only when he needs him; in the other he supports him whether he has work for him or not. . . . . Emancipation enables the master to get more labor and to pay less for it. Emancipation frees the slave from the whip, but deprives him also of his food, and since hungry people have small respect for the laws, he soon discovers that while he escapes the whip he stumbles upon the treadmill or the gallows."

Despite this glaring exposure of the hypocrisy which was really back of the whole middle-class movement in behalf of the emancipation of the slaves, the workingmen of England nevertheless demanded the abolition of Negro slavery, only insisting, like their American class comrades, on the equal necessity of the abolition of white slavery. The workingmen took an active part in the numerous meetings arranged by the middle class anti-slavery societies in England in the thirties and forties in the interest of their cause. The adoption of the Reform Bill (1832) had put the English middle class into political power, but at the same time had set in striking relief the antagonism existing between the middle class and the working class, and inspired the latter to independent action.

In June, 1836, the Working Men's Association, which subsequently played an important part as the mother organization of the Chartist movement, was founded in London. In the fall of

1837 the English press, Tory and Whig alike, teemed with inflammatory attacks against the United States, whose republican institutions were bitterly assailed and ridiculed.   The Working Men's Association resolved to combat the mischievous machinations of the ruling class.   The carpenter, William Lovett, who in the following year outlined the "People's Charter," those six points embodying the demands of the workingmen which gave the Chartist movement its name, was entrusted by the Working Men's Association with the composition of a manifesto in which the inflammatory attacks of the middle-class press were to be answered and the existing prejudices neutralized as far as possible.

The manifesto began with an allusion to the spirit of fraternity which should govern workingmen in all the countries of the world:

"For, as the subjugation and misery of our class can be traced to our ignorance and dissensions—as the knaves and hypocrites of the world live by our follies, and the tyrants of the world are strong because we, the working millions, are divided—so assuredly will the mutual instruction and united exertions of our class in all countries rapidly advance the world's emancipation."

In this address the English workingmen called the attention of the working classes in America to the fact that within the borders of their country millions of human beings were held as slaves, because their skins were not white, but black. The part of the manifesto which alluded to chattel slavery was as follows:

"With no disposition either to question your political sincerity, impugn your morality or to upbraid you for vices you did not originate, it is with feelings of regret, brethren, that we deem it is even needed to enquire of men who for more than half a century have had the power of government in their hands, why the last and blackest remnant of kingly dominion has not been uprooted from republican America?

"Why, when she has afforded a home and an asylum for the destitute and oppressed among all nations, should oppression in her own land be legalized, and bondage tolerated? Did nature, when she cast her sunshine o'er the earth, and adapted her children to its influence, intend that her varied tints of skin should be the criterion of liberty? And shall men, whose illustrious ancestors proclaimed mankind to be brothers by nature, make an exception to degrade to the condition of slaves, human beings a shade darker than themselves?

"Surely it cannot be for the interest of the working classes that these prejudices should be fostered—this degrading traffic be maintained. No! No! It must be for those who shrink from honest industry, and who would equally sacrifice, to their love of gain and mischievous ambition, the happiness of either *black* or *white*. We entertain the opinion, friends, that those who seek to consign you to unremitting toil, to fraudulently monopolize your lands, to cheat you in the legislature, to swell your territory by injustice, and to keep you ignorant and divided, are the same persons who are the perpetuators and advocates of slavery.

"They are rich and powerful, we judge from their corruptive influence; for, with few honest exceptions, that surest guarantee of liberty, *the press,* is diverted to their purpose and subject to their power, instead of performing its sacred office in developing truth, and in extirpating the errors of mankind and—shame to their sacred calling—-there are *preachers* and *teachers* and *learned men* among you, who plead eloquently against the foibles of the poor, but shrink from exposing vice in high stations—nay, *who are even the owners of slaves, and the abettors and advocates of slavery!"*

In the same manifesto the English workingmen expatiate also on the regrettable fact that the workingmen of the United States do not understand the democratic principles of their Charter of Independence to that extent "which it becomes you to understand them." Further, in showing what the working class of England was trying to do for the betterment of its "degrading condition," the address says:

"Seeing the result of our ignorance and divisions, subjecting us to be tools of party, the slaves of power, and the victims of our own dissipations and vices, we have resolved to unite and *mutually instruct ourselves;* and, as a means to that end we have formed ourselves into workingmen's associations. . . . ."

". . . . And we would respectfully urge you to enquire whether similar means might not be more advantageously and extensively employed in your country."*

That the Chartist papers in the forties declared themselves against Negro slavery in the United States, we have already learned from the controversy between Feargus O'Connor of the *Northern Star* in Leeds and George H. Evans of the *Working Men's Advocate* in New York, in which, from a historical point of view, the English Chartist leader proved himself superior in insight and clearness of conception to the American National Reformer. The remaining organs of the English Chartist press also ranged themselves bravely against slavery in America.

In 1846 an Anti-Slavery League, whose membership was composed principally of English radical workingmen and whose president was the Chartist George Thompson, was formed in Lon-

---

* William Lovett: *Life and Struggles.* London, 1876, pp. 131-134.

don. Among the members of the League were also William Lovett and many other well-known followers and champions of the Chartist movement. This association was formed when William Lloyd Garrison, Frederick Douglas, and Henry C. Wright, all three very active Abolitionists, visited England. The chief object of their visit was to impress upon religious bodies that slavery was a heinous sin and ought to be abolished; and also to urge on them the necessity of withholding fellowship from the religious bodies of America which were the advocates and abettors of slavery. Among other religious bodies in England and Scotland they endeavored to influence the Evangelical Alliance, but were unsuccessful. They called a public meeting on the subject at Exetor Hall, where the Christianity of the Evangelical Alliance was exposed. The Workingmen's Anti-Slavery League condemned in strong terms the conduct of these Christian bodies, which, for the sake of filthy lucre, and the subscriptions they were in the habit of receiving from the religious Christian slaveholders of America, persisted in recognizing them, regardless of the millions of their fellow-men in slavery.

The Anti-Slavery League employed and paid Frederick Douglas for a time as an agitator for the anti-slavery cause, and he and the president of the League, George Thompson, made extended trips throughout the land and called forth great sympathy in behalf of the slaves.*

As we see, Garrison and his Abolitionist friends met with the same experience in their encounters with Christian ministers and similar middle-class elements which they had made at the beginning of their agitation in New England. They found themselves opposed by enemies where they had hoped to find friends, and they found friends of their cause among the working class who had to fight slavery within their own ranks.

The organized workingmen of England continued their resolute opposition to slavery also in the following decade. In the numerous meetings called by the anti-slavery societies it was especially the workingmen who again and again protested against the preservation of slavery. The labor organizations also frequently took a similar position, and in May, 1853, George Jacob Holyoake sent an anti-slavery address from the Democrats of England to the Democrats of the United States. This address was signed by about 1,800 men, all prominent among the workers and their organizations in England.

More emphatically than even the free workingmen of the North of the United States, both American and German, did the workingmen of

---

* Lovett, p. 321.

England raise their voice against slavery during the whole period of the agitation. Although, or perhaps because, they were at that time themselves in a condition which can be truly described as white slavery, they did not in their own dependence forget that of the poor blacks, who, bound to the soil and to their masters, were compelled to bear the twofold burden of the oppressed class and the oppressed race.

We shall see later how nobly the workingmen of England during the Civil War redeemed the promise of their attitude in the anti-slavery movement. The narrative dealing with this attitude covers one of the most glorious pages in the history of the labor movement.

CHAPTER III.

FREE LABOR BEFORE THE SENATE OF THE UNITED STATES.

The relations between the labor question and the question of Negro slavery, and the economic antagonisms necessarily engendered by industrial development between free workmen and capitalists, were well recognized by the slaveholders, and played no inconsiderable part in the arguments advanced by the latter in defence of slavery.

The awakening class consciousness, as it manifested itself in the early years of the organized labor movement, gave workingmen a certain caution and reserve in their judgment concerning slavery and Negro emancipation. This caution and reserve were the more pronounced the more forcibly class consciousness made itself felt among them.

The slaveholders promptly saw and recognized in the rising labor movement the enemy which free capital was nursing. They foresaw the inevitable conflict which had to arise between workingmen and capitalists in consequence of the removal of all barriers against industry based on

free competition.   They sought to exploit for
their own advantage the antagonism between free
workingmen and capitalists which they had fore-
seen.   They warned the anti-slavery capitalists of
the North against this development and the consequences which it would have for them.   They
saw in the maintenance of slavery the true solution of the social question and the chief defence
against the social dangers raised by this question
and the movement of free workingmen in general, and they appealed to the industrial capitalists not to overlook this danger in their campaign against the Negro slavery of the South.

On March 4, 1858, James H. Hammond,
United States Senator from South Carolina and
one of the most rabid champions of Negro
slavery, took the floor of the Senate in reply to
a speech delivered the day before by Senator
Seward of New York.   He said, among other
things:

"The Senator from New York said yesterday
that the whole world had abolished slavery.   Aye,
the *name,* but not the thing; all the powers of the
earth cannot abolish it.   God only can do it when
he repeals the fiat, 'the poor ye always have with
you'; for the man who lives by daily labor, and
scarcely lives at that, and who has to put out his
labor in the market and take the best he can get
for it—in short, your whole hireling class of
manual laborers and 'operatives,' as you call them,

are essentially slaves. The difference between us is, that our slaves are hired for life and well compensated; there is no starvation, no begging, no want of employment among our people, and not too much employment either. Yours are hired by the day, not cared for, and scantily compensated which may be proved in the most painful manner at any hour, in any street, in any of your large towns. Why, you meet more beggars in one day, in any single street of the city of New York, than you would meet in a lifetime in the whole South. We do not think that whites should be slaves, either by law or necessity. Our slaves are black, of another and inferior race. The status in which we have placed them is an elevation. They are elevated from a condition in which God first created them, by being made our slaves. None of that race on the whole face of the globe can be compared with the slaves of the South. They are happy, content, unaspiring, and utterly incapable, from intellectual weakness, ever to give any trouble by their aspirations.

"Your slaves are white, of your own race: you are brothers of one blood. They are your equals in natural endowment of intellect, and they feel galled by their degradation. Our slaves do not vote. We give them no political power. Yours do vote; and being the majority, they are the depositaries of all your political power. If they knew the tremendous secret, that the ballot-box is stronger than an army with bayonets, and could combine, where would you be? Your society would be reconstructed, your government over-thrown, your property divided, not as they have mistakenly attempted to initiate such proceedings by meetings in parks, with arms in their hands, but by the quiet process of the ballot-box. You have been making war upon us to our very hearth-stones. How would you like us to send lecturers or agitators North, to teach these people this, to aid and assist in combining, and to lead them?"*

Hammond's description of the idyllic social conditions in the South had no foundation in truth. But this did not preclude the clever Sen-ator of South Carolina from hitting the nail on the head in everything relating to the develop-ment of the social relations between capital and workingmen under the capitalistic régime, as his-tory has since proved. His point of view was purely demagogical, but his vision of the future was clearly and sharply defined. Not only the Northern capitalists, but the Northern working-men, might have learned from him, and as far as the latter are concerned they might well heed his words even to-day.

Hammond's speech made a sensation. It is possible that the party of the slaveholders at least partially made good its threat to send agitators to

---

* *Congressional Globe.* U. S. Senate, 1858, p. 962.

the North to teach workingmen there the doctrines elucidated by Hammond. In various labor
papers in the North that part of his speech which
related to the labor question and to the antagonism existing between capital and labor was re-
printed and commented upon in his spirit. The
more independent the movement of any fraction
or nationality or trade of the working class had
become, the more its members were convinced
of the correctness of the arguments of the Senator from South Carolina. These workingmen
already knew that they would owe the improvement of their lot and their deliverance only to the
incessant struggle against capitalist society. But
their historical sense was not yet sufficiently developed to cause them to understand that there
could be no solution of the social question, no
deliverance of "free labor," nay, not even a
powerful labor movement in America, without a
previous solution of the slavery question. This
explains that approval with which Hammond's
speech met among them under the influence of
agitators paid by the slaveholders.

The sensation which Hammond's speech had
made in the public forced the representatives of
the North in the Senate to reply to it. The task
devolved upon Henry Wilson, one of the Senators from Massachusetts, who replied on March
20, 1858. Hammond's statements relating to the
social conditions in the South had been the weak-

est part of his speech. It was easy for the Senator from Massachusetts to set them right. "The Senator tells us," declared Wilson, "that their slaves are well compensated. The Senator himself stated, that a field hand could be supported for from eighteen to nineteen dollars per annum. Is that well compensated? There is not a poorhouse in the free States, where there would not be a rebellion in three days, if the inmates were compelled to subsist on the quantity of food the Senator estimates as ample 'compensation' for the labor of a slave in South Carolina. Wages in the North are 100 per cent. higher than in the South. In the iron mills in Massachusetts, they paid the laborers (1850) $30 a month; in South Carolina the workingmen of the same occupation received but $15."

It was easy to convict the South Carolina Senator of misrepresenting the social conditions of the South, but it was difficult to refute his statements concerning capitalist development and its consequences for free workingmen. And the fact is that his opponent from Massachusetts, in his answer, hardly got beyond mere phrases. It was evident that he did not grasp the antagonism existing between capital and labor, which Hammond had depicted so clearly, and that he did not see the impending conflict between free workingmen and industrial capitalists. "The Senator from South Carolina," explained Wilson, "exclaims, 'the man who lives by daily labor, your whole class of manual laborers, are essentially slaves,'—'they feel galled by their degradation!' What sentiment is this to hear uttered in the councils of this democratic Republic! These words brand hundreds of thousands of men as 'slaves.'

"I, too, have lived by daily labor. I, too, have been a 'hireling manual laborer,' but I never felt 'galled by my degradation.'

"I tell the Senator from South Carolina, that he grossly libels the hireling class of manual laborers, when he declares, that they are 'essentially slaves.'"

And, after showing the real condition of the South, Wilson continued:

"The laboring men of the free States have open to their industry all the avenues of agriculture, commerce, manufactures and the multifarious mechanic arts, where skilled labor is demanded, and where they have not to maintain, as in South Carolina, 'a feeble and ruinous competition with the labor of slaves.'

"Should the Senator and his agitators and lecturers come to Massachusetts, to teach our hireling class of manual laborers 'the secret of the ballot-box,' they would reply: 'We are free men; we are the peers of the gifted and the wealthy; we know the tremendous secret of the ballot-box; and we mould and fashion these institutions that

bless and adorn our proud and free Common-
wealth!" .... "Go home, say to your privileged
class, which you vauntingly say, 'leads progress,
civilization, and refinement,' that it is the opinion
of the hireling laborers of Massachusetts, if you
have no sympathy for your African bondmen, in
whose veins flows so much of your own blood,
you should at least sympathize with the millions of
your own race, whose labor you have dishonored
and degraded by slavery! You should teach your
millions of poor and ignorant white men, so long
oppressed by your policy, the 'tremendous secret,
that the ballot-box is stronger than an army with
banners!' You should combine and lead them to
the adoption of a policy which shall secure their
own emancipation from a degrading thrall-
dom!"*

The Senator from Massachusetts did not know
the history of the workingmen in his own State.
Otherwise he would have known that notwithstanding all their hatred of the system of
slavery in the South and notwithstanding
all their enthusiasm for the emancipation
of the Negroes, the workingmen of Massachusetts had always, when they met in organizations, emphasized the fact that besides the abolition of Negro slavery they also demanded the
abolition of wage slavery. Otherwise he would
have known that industrial workingmen, as soon

---

* *Congressional Globe.* U. S. Senate, 1858.

as they begin to think about their condition, do not at all feel as "free men, as peers of the gifted and wealthy," but that they are conscious of living in a slavery hardly inferior to that of the Negroes of the South, and that they wanted deliverance from *all* slavery, the chattel slavery of the Negroes and the wage slavery of the white workingmen.

All this the Senator from Massachusetts would have known had he been familiar with the history of labor in his own State. At that moment, of course, the workingmen of Massachusetts like those of the North in general were condemned to remain silent. The terrible crisis of 1857 had destroyed their organizations, so far as there had been any, and annihilated their press, what there was of it. And in March, 1858, when this debate took place in the United States Senate, the labor movement had not yet recovered from the blows it had received.

Otherwise workingmen from the ranks of his own State might have told the Senator from Massachusetts that he knew less about the social conditions of their class than did the Senator from South Carolina, and that Senator Hammond was right when he said to the capitalists of the North, "Your whole hireling class of manual laborers and 'operatives,' as you call them, are essentially slaves."

That this was the opinion of the advanced por-

tion of the workingmen of his State, Senator
Wilson might easily have learned from the anti-
slavery press of Massachusetts, the press of his
own party. Although the influence of the real
social reformers upon the working class of the
North had materially diminished in the fifties,
and the necessity of abolishing wage slavery was
no longer emphasized as strongly as formerly, a
workingman wrote in Garrison's *Liberator* in
September, 1860, shortly before the outbreak of
the Civil War, as follows:

"Let us deprecate Southern slavery in the
depths of our souls; but, in the name of Heaven,
don't let us be unmindful of this other form of
slavery, equally the result of dire selfishness,
manifesting itself in a greater degree than ever
in the overtopping, all-absorbing, bargaining and
trading spirit of this age—the one accomplished
by man-stealing, the other the outbirth of a false
relation existing in the great department of
labor."*

The feeling that they were not free men was
evidently not yet extinct in the working class of
Massachusetts.

---

* *Liberator,* Sept. 14, 1860.

CHAPTER IV.

THE OUTBREAK OF THE CIVIL WAR AND THE LABOR MOVEMENT.

1. General Condition of the Labor Movement.

The economic crisis of 1857 had struck a severe blow at the feeble beginnings of the labor movement in the United States. There existed trade organizations, and even national organizations of some trades—for example, those of the printers and the hatters—but they had no great influence, and they were unable to withstand such blows as those dealt by the prevailing crisis.

The weakness of the American trade-union movement at that time was due to the relatively insignificant industrial development of the country. Capitalist industry on a large scale existed really only in three of the New England States, in Massachusetts, Rhode Island and Connecticut. Industrial workers, in the present sense, were therefore to be found only in those regions. The farmers made up the bulk of the population. Industrial products were for the most part manufactured in the manner of the old trades by handicraftsmen. There were proportionately few

Americans among the mechanics. Owing to their knowledge of the country and its language they could more easily find employment in agriculture, in trading and in commerce than in the factory and the workshop, at least outside of the three New England States just named. Unskilled labor was principally supplied by Irish immigrants, while the mechanic trades were supplied by Germans. The trade organizations of German workingmen consequently formed a much more important part of the general labor movement at that time than they did later. In correspondence with the industrial development all labor organizations of the time reflected somewhat the character of artisan gilds. These trade unions, where they continued to exist, were only gradually transformed into organizations of modern industrial workingmen.

It was almost two years before the labor organizations recovered from the effects of the crisis of 1857. Then they showed renewed activity. Local organizations, both German and English, were formed in all the large cities, and national trade federations came into existence. The iron and steel workers took the initiative by forming a national federation under the name "Sons of Vulcan." In March, 1859, at a convention in Philadelphia, the machinists and blacksmiths followed; in July, in the same city, the iron molders. In the following year, in 1860, there were already twenty-six trades with national organizations.* Of these national trade organizations which were formed shortly before the outbreak of the Civil War, those of the machinists and blacksmiths and those of the iron molders are of special interest, because they were under the influence of persons who subsequently played an important part in the labor movement of America.

In the spring of 1859 the iron molders of various cities went on strike. The employers refused to agree to the demands of their workmen and formed for the Eastern and Middle States a national organization, The National Founders' League. This employers' organization tried to import workingmen from foreign countries and thus break the strike. There was one workingman of that trade, William H. Sylvis of Philadelphia, who saw through the scheme of the employers and resolved to work against them. He attempted to unite the several local organizations of the trade in order to oppose the national union of the employers by a national union of the workingmen. In consequence of his efforts the Iron Molders' Convention met in Philadelphia on July 5, 1859, and effected a strong organization of the trade.

The convention chose a committee which was to draft an address to the iron molders of the

* Ely: *The Labor Movement*. 1886, p. 60.

United States. This address was written by
Sylvis. It is of interest to-day because it gives
an insight into the conceptions and ideas then
current in the American labor world. Among
other things it said:

"Wealth is power, and practical experience
teaches us that it is a power but too often used
to oppress and degrade the daily laborer. Year
after year the capital of the country becomes
more and more concentrated in the hands of a
few, and, in proportion as the wealth of the country becomes centralized, its power increases, and
the laboring classes are impoverished. It therefore becomes us, as men who have to battle with
the stern realities of life, to look this matter fair
in the face; there is no dodging the question; let
every man give it a fair, full and candid consideration, and then act according to his honest
convictions. *What position are we, the mechanics of America, to hold in society?* Are we to
receive an equivalent for our labor sufficient to
maintain us in comparative independence and re-
spectability, to procure the means with which to
educate our children, and qualify them to play
their part in the world's drama; or must we be
forced to bow the suppliant knee to wealth, and
earn by unprofitable toil a life of solace to confirm the very chains that bind us to our doom?"*

Life, Speeches, Labors and Essays of Wm. H. Sylvis,
by his brother, James C. Sylvis, 1872, p. 31.

Emphasizing the fact that the power of the workingmen lies in organization, Sylvis urged his colleagues to join the new union.

At the convention of his national union, held at Albany, N. Y., in 1860, the author of this address, who even at that time brought out clearly the relation of the workingmen to capital, was appointed a leading officer in the organization, and as such played an important part not only in his union, but also in the American labor movement in general.

Besides the national union of the iron molders the organizations of the machinists and blacksmiths and of the shipwrights were at that period particularly active. Both trades were even then eagerly discussing the eight-hour day. At the annual convention of the former a demand was made for an eight-hour day legalized by Congress, and the shipwrights in some localities obtained their eight-hour day merely in consequence of their strong organization. In other English-speaking trade unions shortly before the outbreak of the Civil War there was considerable activity, as also in those of the immigrant German workingmen.

The condition of the few independent political labor organizations, which were German, was less encouraging. The anti-slavery agitation and the impending political conflict were a great hindrance to them. The *Arbeiterbund* (Working-

men's League) of New York was more deeply
concerned about wage slavery than about chattel
slavery, and the same thing was true of its organ,
the *Soziale Republik*.   In St. Louis there were
German workingmen's organizations which were
loosely allied with the *Arbeiterbund,* and there
were yet others in Chicago.   Pupils of Karl Marx
still exerted some influence in the Lake City;
most noted among these was Joseph Weydemeyer,   who   edited   a   workingmen's   paper,
Stimme des Volkes, which was published by the
central committee of the German workingmen's
organizations.   The *Soziale Republik* and the
Stimme des Volkes were discontinued in the
course of the year 1860.   The impending conflict
between the slaveholding South and the "free
labor" North crowded out all other questions,
and for the time being made impossible any political labor movement, although the trade unions
were comparatively active.

Such was the state of the labor movement
when the election of Abraham Lincoln in the Fall
of 1860 induced the Southern States to secede
from the Union and thus inaugurate the Civil
War.

2. The Attitude of the Workingmen To-
wards the War.

The outbreak of a war like that between the
North and the South, threatening with destruc-

tion the very foundations of the Union, was bound to react most profoundly upon the industrial activity of the people and concomitantly also upon the labor movement. There was indeed at the beginning of the war a general collapse of all industry, and the labor organizations which had prospered since the close of the year 1858 received a severe setback; many of them even disappeared altogether during the first years of the war.

The attitude of the workingmen towards the War of Secession was by no means uniformly the same. At the beginning the question of slavery played no part; it gave way to the question of the preservation of the Union, whose existence was threatened by the secession of the Southern States. Though the slavery question lay at the foundation of the whole secession movement, the politicians at Washington did their best to obscure the situation by causing the ensuing struggle to appear not as a struggle against the economic institution of Negro slavery, but as a struggle for a political form, the preservation of the Union. And as a struggle for the preservation of the Union the Civil War was at the outset regarded by the labor organizations, though it cannot be said that they hailed it with general enthusiasm. The labor organizations of the South, such as had at that time come into existence in Baltimore and some other cities of the

Southern States, were not at all in favor of the struggle of their States against the Union, and it must be particularly emphasized that they were in the beginning generally in favor of the preservation of the Union and against the secessionist movement of the ruling class of their States.

Some influential representatives of the trade unions, both North and South, endeavored to persuade the laboring class of the country to exert their influence against the war. One of the most active among these was Sylvis. A conference of certain members of the Iron Molders' Union met in Louisville, Ky., and passed resolutions to the effect that workingmen, regardless of their political party affiliations, were convinced that the welfare of the country and the hopes of the future reposed upon the preservation of the Union.* The election of Abraham Lincoln, in their opinion, furnished no grounds for changing the existing form of government.

The resolutions passed at this conference of workingmen in a Southern State further urged the workingmen of the whole country to arrange meetings in every congressional district and there demand the resignation of all those members of Congress at Washington whose attitude was inimical to the preservation of the Union. At the close emphasis was laid on the statement

* Sylvis, p. 42.

that the mechanics of Kentucky were in favor of the preservation of the Union, even if they did not consider themselves its humble subjects. They knew what their rights were, and they were determined to maintain them within or outside of the Union.

Similar meetings were held elsewhere in the South, as well as in the North, by organized workingmen, and similar declarations were made there, all these movements finally culminating in a labor convention at Philadelphia on February 22, 1861. The call for this convention had come from Louisville.

The attendance at this convention was not so great as had been expected, although delegates from many States were present. Sylvis was one of the most active. Uriah S. Stephens, the garment cutter who subsequently became the founder of the Order of the Knights of Labor, was also one of the delegates. It was resolved to appoint a Committee of Thirty-four—one for each of the States then constituting the Union—with the function of arranging meetings and demonstrations in the spirit of the callers of the convention. The proceedings closed with a large parade of workingmen and a mass meeting in which the speakers emphasized the fact that organized labor was willing to sink political differences for the sake of preserving the Union.

Some days previous to the convention, on February 12, Sylvis had expressed his views concerning its tasks in a communication to a workingmen's paper, the *Mechanics' Own* of Philadelphia. After stating that the coming convention was to be a *workingmen's* convention, he declared that "under the leadership of political demagogues and traitors scattered all over the land, North and South, East and West, the country is going to the devil as fast as it can. And unless the masses rise up in their might, and teach their representatives what to do, the good old ship will go to pieces." In this communication he urged the arrangement of meetings in which the preservation of the Union was to be championed.

The Committee of Thirty-four, which had been appointed by the convention at Philadelphia, continued its activity after the close of the proceedings and held several sessions. In a letter of March 23, the corresponding secretary of the committee, Sylvis, expressed himself with regard to its mission as follows:

"The business of this committee is to perfect and perpetuate an organization among the industrial classes of the city and State, for the purpose of placing in positions of public trust men of known honesty and ability; men who know the real wants of the people, and who will represent us according to our wishes; men who have not made politics a trade; men who, for a consideration, will not become the mere tools of rotten corporations and aristocratic monopolies; men who will devote their time and energies to the making of good laws, and direct their administration in such a way as will best subserve the interests of the whole people."*

Simultaneously with the workingmen's convention in Philadelphia a mass meeting of workingmen was held in Faneuil Hall, in Boston, which was still more outspoken in its condemnation of the war. This meeting issued an "Address of the Workingmen of Massachusetts to their Brethren Throughout the United States," in which occur these statements:

"We believe the chief cause of the break in the Union to have been that the people, North and South, have been deceived and betrayed by politicians and office seekers. . . . .

". . . . It is vain for politicians to tell us that secession is illegal. Several States *have* seceded already; and if the citizens of those States are united in their determination to leave the Union, no laws and no force can compel them to remain.

". . . . Since coercion is unwise, unjust and impossible, we must look to other means for the restoration of the Union, and we believe that those means are in the power of the people. Between the people of the States, there can be no misunderstanding if they can be brought together.

---

* Sylvis, pp. 45-46.

"We believe that the first duty of the people, South and North, is to put away forever those designing politicians who have deceived the people and brought the danger upon the country.

"We appeal to our brethren at the South to deal with their traitors at home, the sowers of sedition, who endeavor to mislead and misrepresent them.

"We, on our part, will do our best here at the North to expose and to put down forever the mischief-makers who have sown discord between the States, and brought our country to the verge of civil war."

The address attacks the Abolitionists most violently. Among the reasons given in justification of this attack, are the following:

"Because their pretended love for slaves a thousand miles away is but hypocrisy. If they loved mankind, and would prevent sin and suffering and wrong, they could find here at home objects more than sufficient for the exercise of all their assumed virtues. But their philanthropy is mere deception—their affected sympathy is selfishness—and their feigned love for the slave, a cloak for their insidious designs.

"For these, and for many other reasons, we appeal to all good citizens at the North—Republicans and Democrats, Union Men and Americans—to see to it, that henceforth the pest of Abolition shall under no disguise be tolerated in their councils.

"But to the Republicans we appeal most earnestly, to avow their open hostility, because the Abolitionists have, for their own purpose, deceived the South and taught them to believe that all Republicans are Abolitionists.

"Let this be a war not of force, but of opinion. . . . ."

". . . . The truth is, that the workingmen care little for the strife of political parties and the intrigues of office-seekers. We regard them with the contempt they deserve. We are weary of this question of slavery; it is a matter which does not concern us; and we wish only to attend to our business, and leave the South to attend to their own affairs, without any interference from the North.

". . . . The workingmen of the United States have other duties than to put down the treasonable designs of the Abolitionists. It is in our power to save the Union, if we will but unite. Let us forget, then, forever that we have been Whigs or Democrats, Republicans or Americans, or Union men, and let the symbols and platforms and passions and prejudices of party be discarded, never to be recalled. . . . .

". . . . Let us form throughout the land associations of workingmen, whose only platform shall be, Liberty and Union, and equal rights to all. . . . .

". . . . If our Southern brethren choose to return to the Union, we will give them a sincere and hearty welcome, and endeavor to protect them in their rights. If they prefer to cast their lot with us no longer, we will bid them 'go in peace,' and we will endeavor to secure to ourselves the blessings of liberty and independence in our own government. We wish no Union but a Union of Friendship, not of force; no associates but those who remain with us of their own free will."*

It is probable that this address was not backed exclusively by the workingmen of Boston, but that Democratic political influence was brought to bear in its composition, as the violent attack upon the Abolitionists would seem to indicate. The Abolitionists were indeed far less popular among the workingmen of Boston than among the population of the essentially industrial centres of New England. Nevertheless the address is of interest for the light it sheds upon the attitude of some of the workingmen of the North at the outbreak of the war.

The address of the Workingmen of Boston, as well as the activity of Sylvis and the Committee of Thirty-four, did not of course alter the march of events. The working class of the

---

* *Liberator.* March, 1861.

United States was by no means strongly enough developed to make any impression by setting forth its class interests. And even if the work ingmen had been better organized, if their movement had been more powerfully developed, and if they had constituted a more vital section of society, their action would nevertheless have proved futile, for the simple reason that they entered upon it too late. The State of South Carolina had seceded from the Union as early as December 30, 1860. Five other States had followed its example in the next month. The anti-slavery people in the North and the slaveholding element in the South were alike bent on war, so that the pacific efforts of the poorly organized workingmen were doomed in advance. Calamity, if one may speak of historically necessary struggles as calamity, had to take its course. Already, on April 12th, the Secessionists had fired on Fort Sumter, in Charleston harbor. The War of the Rebellion, which was to lead to the abolition of slavery, had begun.

3.   EFFECTS OF THE WAR ON LABOR.

The first thing to note at the outbreak of the war was the general industrial depression, with its accompanying unemployment, a circumstance which greatly facilitated the organization of the Northern army, as the unemployed willingly enlisted in the ranks. The labor organizations suf-

fered from the prevailing unemployment, and
partly also because their members obeyed the call
for volunteers in such great numbers as to leave
them with a greatly depleted membership. Many
trade-union officials and labor leaders busied
themselves in behalf of reinforcing the army by
recruiting military companies from their organizations and workshops in which they held the
leading positions. A trade-union in Philadelphia joined the army in a body, an action which
was recorded by the following remarks in the
minutes of the Union: "It having been resolved
to enlist with Uncle Sam for the war, this union
stands adjourned until either the Union is safe
or we are whipped."*

The enlistment of so many thousands of workingmen in the army was of course accompanied
by a corresponding decrease in the supply of labor. There soon was no army of unemployed.
To furnish the supplies for the army and navy,
equipment, armament, provisions, clothing, tents,
transports and the manifold other needs of a
large military body, made vast demands on productive labor. The requirements of the army
stimulated prostrate industry, which presently
showed renewed activity in all its branches. Enlarged opportunity of employment gave the workingmen indeed an increase in wages, but hand
in hand with this enlarged opportunity came an-

* T. V. Powderly: *Thirty Years of Labor*, p. 57.

other economic phenomenon which tended to
make their condition worse. War was expen-
sive; it ate up enormous sums. In the year 1861
the amount of money which the Government required for the army and navy was $35,389,000;
in the following year it had risen to $431,813,-
000; and in 1865 it had mounted to $1,153,307,-
000. The war expenses of the North for the five
years of the war (1861-1865) totalled $3,063,-
180,000.* This colossal sum had to be procured. Debts were incurred; recourse was had
to the issue of paper money. But the result of
the war was uncertain, and therefore it was also
uncertain whether the government issuing this
paper money would ever be able to redeem it in
gold to pay its debts. Paper money was depreciated. During the war one dollar in paper was
worth only from forty to seventy cents in gold.
The consequence was a general increase in the
price of commodities amounting on the average
to 75 per cent. In some cases the price was
tripled in the years between 1860 and 1866.
Wages were of course paid in depreciated paper
money.

This movement in commodity prices resulting
from the depreciation of paper money put the
American workingmen into such a position that
in spite of a favorable labor market they were

---

* Katherine Coman: *Industrial History of the United
States*, p. 270.

worse off than before. It forced them into a
struggle for the maintenance of their standard of
life; they set forth new demands; their failing
organizations began to revive, and new ones were
formed. The war rebuilt what it had previously
destroyed. The labor movement once more became a powerful factor in public life.

Besides the struggle of the workingmen for
the maintenance of their standard of life, and
besides the increased demand for labor during
the years of the war, there was still another factor to influence favorably the revival of the labor movement. While the wage worker, in spite
of a favorable labor market, was compelled to
struggle for the maintenance of the prevailing
standard of life, the middle classes of the North
were revelling in "orgies of profit." Under the
fructifying rain of millions which the Government spent in liquidation of army and navy contracts and supplies, industry on a large scale began to develop and consolidate by leaps and
bounds. Mass production of the articles required
by the army resulted in transforming all workshops into factories. The various concerns were
enormously enlarged, concentrating the workingmen in large numbers in individual factories.
About this time hand work was replaced by the
use of machines in nearly all industries. There
was an accumulation of wealth in individual
hands hitherto unheard of. Dishonest manipu-

lations of army contractors—we need recall only the clothing manufactured out of old woolen "shoddy," and footgear similarly produced— poured millions into the pockets of a few "shoddy aristocrats," as did also the fitting out of "blockade runners" which carried merchandise between ports declared closed. Legislation, and especially Congressional legislation, became a tool in the hands of the middle class to a greater extent than had ever been the case before. Millions of acres of government lands were granted to railroad companies and other monopolies. Capitalism gloried in unparalleled successes. The national wealth of the United States, which in 1860 had been $514 per capita, had risen in 1870 to $780, despite the colossal destruction of property in consequence of the war, from which the Southern States were the principal sufferers. It was especially in the industrial districts of New England, in New York, and other large cities of the Northeastern States that we meet with these vast accumulations of wealth. In the Northern Atlantic States the national wealth amounted to $528 per capita in 1860, or only $14 above the average of the whole country. In 1870, in the same section, it had risen to $1,243 per capita, or $463 above the average. Here in the Northeastern section of the country the foundation was laid, during the

Civil War, for the money power of the United States.

The extraordinary rapidity with which the process of capitalist consolidation took place in the hothouse atmosphere of the war was of course accompanied by the creation at the same pace of the soil out of which sprang the labor movement. The first indication of this was seen in the rise everywhere of local trade unions and their subsequent federation into national organizations. As early as 1863 the locomotive engineers formed an organization which embraced the entire country, and in the following year the cigarmakers and bricklayers did likewise. At the close of the war between thirty and forty trades had formed national organizations in the United States.

CHAPTER V.

ABRAHAM LINCOLN AND THE WORKING CLASS.

1. The English Workingmen and the Civil War.

Of the European countries, it was especially England that was affected by the outbreak of the Civil War. As we have seen, England was connected with the Southern States by a bond of common interests. Its textile industry, which had reached its highest development towards the close of the fifties, needed the raw cotton of the cultivation of which the Southern States possessed a monopoly. The latter, owing to the institution of slavery, were interested in the importation of English products free of duty, while the young manufacturing industry of the North favored a protective policy which found actual expression in the national tariff laws. It was consequently in the interest of the English middle class that the Southern States should form an independent confederacy with tariff regulations of its own which should grant England undisturbed free trade. Under such an arrangement the

South could supply England with the raw cotton which was so necessary to it, and English manufacturers could export their industrial products of all kinds to the Southern States, free of duty, and without fear of competition. Under the pressure of these interests the early Abolitionist impulses of the ruling class in England disappeared, and English intervention in favor of the Southern States was advocated in these circles.

Besides England, France also was interested in the events taking place in the United States. Textile industry was of course far less developed in the Second Empire than in Great Britain, and cotton did not play as important a role in French politics as in English. Nevertheless, French textile workers were also affected by the scarcity of cotton and suffered severely from the crisis produced thereby. But although their distress was due to the War of Secession, like their English comrades they stood by the Union and opposed Negro slavery, and by no means shared their ruler's bias in favor of the Southern slaveholders. On the contrary, they took a very decided stand against them.

It was, however, not the part which the cotton famine and all it involved played in France that drove the French Emperor to sympathize with the South. Louis Napoleon was filled with the lust of conquest and aggrandizement. He had designs upon Mexico that could scarcely be realized if the United States remained intact, and for this reason he sided with the Southern States. He would gladly have made the attempt to break the blockade of the Southern ports proclaimed by the Washington Government, and he would even have directly intervened in favor of the South, had he not feared thereby to involve France in conflicts of far-reaching consequences. For this reason, he desired the co-operation of England in this enterprise, and he did his best to obtain it.

In England the Government was far more dependent on public opinion than in France. If public opinion in Great Britain had really demanded the recognition of the Southern Confederacy, if it had demanded active intervention in its favor, the Government would only too willingly have obeyed the pressure. But in the face of public opinion emphatically opposed to all intervention on the part of England in the affairs of America, the Government dared not pursue a contrary course. The decision consequently lay with England.

Only a few years had passed since England, on the occasion of the visit of Harriet Beecher Stowe, the author of *Uucle Tom's Cabin,* the book which graphically described the sufferings of Negro slaves, melted in sentimental approval, especially since the author was the honored guest

in the most exclusive circles of the English nobility.   After the outbreak of the Civil War not
a trace of this sentiment remained in the hearts
of the English middle class.   "To-day [1862]
we find only here and there one among the Englishmen who does not fanatically side with the
slave States, and that one probably has not the
courage to express his opinions."*   This was true
as far as the ruling classes were concerned, and
they indeed tried their best to persuade the Government to intervene in behalf of the South.
They arranged labor demonstrations and meetings declaring in favor of the South and of open
hostilities against the North for the purpose of
showing that these sentiments had the backing
of English "public opinion."   But under the influence of persons, many of whom subsequently
belonged to the General Council of the International Workingmen's Association, the workingmen of England offered the most determined opposition to the attempt of forcing them into
demonstrations favoring the slaveholders.   English workingmen had themselves become only too
well acquainted with slavery to espouse its support in one of its most aggravated forms.

The manufacturers now resorted to intimidation to compel the workingmen to join in the

---

* Lothar Bucher: *Die Londoner Industrieausstellung von
1862*.   Berlin, 1863, p. 155.   Bucher evidently considered
only the ruling class as "Englishmen."

cry for war. Starvation, that ever ready weapon in the hands of the middle class, was to force the workingmen of England to declare for slavery in America and thereby enable the Government to say that public opinion demanded its hostile intervention in behalf of the South. The Civil War, and especially the blockade of the Southern ports by Northern forces, had created a scarcity of cotton in England which, by the way, was not altogether unwelcome to the manufacturers. For there had been an overproduction in the cotton industry of England in 1860. "Its effects were still felt during the years immediately following. . . . . The demand for labor had in consequence already been decreased here [in Blackburn, where in 1860 there were 30,000 mechanical looms], months before the effects of the cotton blockade made themselves felt. . . . . The stock on hand [of the manufacturers] of course rose in price as long as it lasted, and the alarming depreciation which ordinarily inevitably accompanies such crises was thus avoided."*

A temporary closing of factories thus sent up the prices of the accumulated commodities, a situation by no means deprecated by the cotton lords, especially since they cherished the hope that starvation would speedily cause the workingmen to adopt the views of the manufacturers in re-

---

* *Report on Factories.* October, 1862, pp. 28-29. Quoted by Karl Marx: *Kapital,* III., 1, p. 106.

gard to the Civil War in America. So the textile factories in the north of England were shut
down. More than half of the looms and
spindles were idle. The wages of the spinners and weavers who continued to be employed
were artificially and forcibly reduced in a manner which literally led to starvation. The manufacturers deliberately increased the misery into
which the workingmen had been thrown by the
scarcity of cotton, hoping thus to drive them to
despair and to demand the Government's intervention in the American troubles. For, as the
middle-class organs declared, the intervention of
England would put an end to their misery.

And this misery of the workingmen, especially in the textile districts of Lancashire, was
indeed alarming. In 1863, when conditions had
already somewhat improved, the weekly wages
of weavers and spinners amounted to 3s. 4d. and
5s. 1d. Despite this low rate, these wages were
still further reduced, particularly by fines. In
1862 weavers' wages ranged from 2s. 6d. per
week up.

"No wonder that, in some parts of Lancashire,
a kind of famine fever broke out.* . . . . But
the working-people had to suffer not only from
the experiments of the manufacturers inside the
mills, and of the municipalities outside; not only
from reduced wages and absence of work, from

---

* Marx: *Capital*, I., p. 283.

want and from charity, and from the eulogistic speeches of Lords and Commons. Unfortunate females who, in consequence of the cotton famine, were at its commencement thrown out of employment, and have thereby become outcasts of society, and now, though trade has revived and work is plentiful, continue members of that unfortunate class, and are likely to continue so. There are also in the borough more youthful prostitutes than I have known for the last 25 years."*

The workingmen of England were starving with exemplary patience. They saw their daughters drift into a life of shame while hunger-typhus decimated their own ranks, but they would not yield to the demands of the brutal factory lords. Not only did they refuse to fall into line with the wishes of their masters and declare themselves in favor of the South, but on the contrary they declared themselves as distinctly against such a policy. The workingmen of England never had better leaders than at this period, and on these leaders' advice they espoused the cause of the abolition of Negro slavery and protested against the intervention of the Government in favor of the South.

Hardly had Lincoln, after more than a year of cautious dealing with the slavery question,

---

*Report on Factories. October 31, 1865. Quoted by Marx: Capital, I., p. 283.

intimated that the War of Secession might be transformed into a war of Negro emancipation, than the workingmen of England, in hundreds of public meetings all over the country, in all industrial sections and large cities, hailed this move with enthusiasm and demanded the initiation of energetic measures against slavery and the slaveholders. In vain were the sneers with which the English ruling class commented on the early defeats of the Union army, in vain was the hypocritical attitude of Gladstone and his colleagues in the Government who sought to disguise their secret desire for intervention by the declaration that the Union could never suppress the Rebellion and that the Civil War meant only useless and aimless bloodshed. Cheerfully, even enthusiastically, the English workingmen bore starvation and misery, and protested more and more loudly against Negro slavery and against the intervention of their Government in favor of the Southern rebels.

In the north of the country, in the cotton districts, where the manufacturers attempted to coerce their employees by starvation, one of the active agitators in favor of the Union was Ernest Jones, the champion and poet of the Chartist movement. His eloquence was irresistible, and his speeches against the slaveholders were so impressive that the towns of Ashton and Rockdale had them printed and circulated at their own expense. When Jones, before a crowded mass meeting at Blackburn, surrounded by the hostile local manufacturers on the platform, exclaimed, "Why did the South secede?" one of the latter replied, "For free trade," whereupon the speaker instantly retorted, "Free trade in what? Free trade in the lash—free trade in the branding iron—free trade in chains."*

The applause which broke forth from the assembled workingmen need not be described. The glowing eloquence of Jones contributed its share in inspiring the starving textile workers of Lancashire to persist in their position.

Let us compare now with the heroism of the workingmen of England the contemptible hypocrisy of the middle class and its leaders. The same Gladstone who declared the attempts of the North to suppress the rebellion of the slaveholders to be futile, and who only waited for an opportunity to bring about an intervention of England in favor of the Southern States, this same Gladstone declared in a speech that the whole history of the Christian church could not furnish so brilliant an example of Christian resignation as that of the workingmen of Lancashire.† Of course, this "Christian resignation" and the exemplary patience of these workingmen were easily explained. Mr. Gladstone him-

---

* Frederick Leary: *Ernest Jones.* London, 1887, p. 72.
† Bucher, pp. 156-57.

self would have them, had they become impatient, imprisoned and shot to pieces amid the applause of the manufacturers, who were responsible for all the misery.

In New York a committee was formed for the purpose of collecting money for the starving spinners and weavers in the north of England and thus alleviating their misery. The "suffering factory workers" of Blackburn addressed a letter to this committee and "to the inhabitants of the United States" beseeching them to furnish the means for their emigration to the United States. But the starving workingmen of the north of England were of far greater use to the Northern capitalists by remaining where they were and continuing to starve and heroically to protest against the machinations of their masters than by coming to the United States. So money was indeed sent to relieve their immediate distress, but Brother Jonathan lent a deaf ear to their entreaties for emigration on a large scale.

The workingmen of England could count even less upon the encouragement of the ruling class of their own country in their plans for emigration. The great mass of the textile workers was indeed without employment at the time, but the manufacturers desired to retain the skilled laborers until they should need them again. On March 24, 1863, a manufacturer declared in the London *Times:*

"Encourage or allow the working-power to emigrate, and what of the capitalists? . . . . Take away the cream of the workers, and fixed capital will depreciate in a great degree, and the floating will not subject itself to a struggle with the short supply of inferior labor. . . . . We are told the workers wish it [emigration]. Very natural it is that they should do so. . . . . Reduce, compress the cotton trade by taking away its working-power and reducing their wages expenditure, say one fifth, or five millions, and what then would happen to the class above, the small store-keepers, and what of the rents—the cottage rents? . . . . Trace out the effects upward to the small farmer, the better householder, and . . . . the land-owner, and say if there could be any suggestion more suicidal, to all classes of the country, than by enfeebling a nation by exporting the best of its manufacturing population, and destroying the value of some of its most productive capital and enrichment "*

The manufacturers' cry of despair found willing ears. The emigration of the workingmen was prevented. "Parliament did not vote a single farthing in aid of emigration, but simply passed some acts empowering the municipal corporations to keep the operatives in a half-starved state

---

* Marx : *Capital,* I., pp. 362-363.

—*i. e.,* to exploit them at less than the normal wages." *

The municipalities ordered public works. The unemployed were set to work on drainage, roads, stone cutting, paving, etc., and drew relief from the local authorities. This action virtually amounted to a relief of the manufacturers, whose skilled hands were kept in the country. Thus "the manufacturer, in secret understanding with the Government. prevented emigration as far as possible, partly in order to have instantly available their capital which consisted in the flesh and blood of these workmen, and partly in order to be sure of the rent which these workmen paid them."†

Many of the manufacturers owned the houses in which the workingmen employed by them were living. Rent could not be paid during the time there was no work. The unpaid rent would have been a pure loss if the workingmen had succeeded in realizing their plan for emigration. Another reason which induced the manufacturers to oppose the scheme with all the means at their disposal was the fact that it offered the workingmen an opportunity of escape from their wretched conditions.

The heroic attitude of the textile workers of England during the Civil War in America con-

---

* Marx: *Capital*, I., p. 364.
† Marx: *Kapital*, III., I., pp. 111-115.

stitutes one of the most glorious pages in the history of the working class and must therefore be emphasized here. They suffered, starved and even died for the cause of Negro emancipation in America. And yet a little less patience would in this case have made the workingmen even more heroic. But the spirit of the Chartists had passed, and the workingmen of England were now great only in passive resistance. The perfidy of the ruling class never challenged instant active resistance more than did the conduct of the English manufacturers and the English government at the time of the Civil War.

The meetings protesting against a war in favor of the Southern States had in the meantime been continued. It was especially during the late winter of 1862 and of 1863 that one such meeting followed another. Above all others the workingmen of London began to be aroused. The trade unions of the metropolis called a meeting at St. James Hall for March 26th which was of special importance, and the declarations of which were recognized as the expression of English working class opinion. At this meeting a prominent part was played by W. R. Cremer, then a cabinet-maker, subsequently a member of the General Council of the International Workingmen's Association, and still later one of the champions of the international peace movement. John Bright was in the chair, and among the speakers were John Stuart Mill and Prof. E. S. Beesly. In an address to Abraham Lincoln which was drawn up by this monster meeting this passage occurs:

"Though we have felt proud of our country . . . . yet have we ever turned with glowing admiration to your great Republic, where a higher political and social freedom has been established."

And John Bright declared:

"I am persuaded . . . . that the more perfect the friendship that is established between the people of England and the free people of America, the more you will find your path of progress here made easy for you, and the more will social and political liberty advance among us."*

Lord Palmerston, then at the head of the English Government, was about to declare war against the Union. According to the testimony of Karl Marx it was this monster meeting of the English trade unions, together with the general attitude of the English working class in the matter, that prevented him from carrying out his intention. The Northern States of America have to thank the working class of England that at that trying period in their conflict with the South they were not involved in an additional war with England, and perhaps also with France.

---

* Henry Bryan Binns: *Abraham Lincoln*. London, 1907.

which would have seriously imperilled the existence of the Union.

2. ABRAHAM LINCOLN AND THE WORKINGMEN OF ENGLAND.

Near the end of September, 1862, Lincoln issued a proclamation to the effect that on January 1, 1863, he would declare free all slaves in those States which should then be in rebellion against the United States and refuse to lay down their arms.

It was natural for the ruling classes of the South to ignore this proclamation. The Southern States had been enabled to maintain a few good privateers for injuring Northern commerce, aided and encouraged therein mainly by England, its nobility, shipbuilders and merchants, with the Government's tacit approval. The slaveholders had every reason to expect that the English ruling classes would lend the Confederacy still further assistance.

But as we have seen, the English working class put in its veto here. The proclamation by Lincoln of his intention to abolish slavery by January 1st called forth great rejoicing; and although there was heard here and there a note of disappointment because the abolition of slavery was put forth as a war measure and not as an unconditional condemnation of slavery on principle, great demonstrations of workingmen took place, alike in the north and the south of England. In meetings at London and at Manchester it was resolved to send an address to President Lincoln expressing the thanks of the English workingmen for the Emancipation Proclamation and encouraging him in taking still more decisive steps. Both meetings took place December 31, 1862.

The address adopted by the London meeting read as follows:

"The Workingmen of London to the President of the United States of America.

"To His Excellency, Abraham Lincoln, President of the United States of America.

"Sir: We who offer this address are Englishmen and workingmen. We prize as our dearest inheritance, bought for us by the blood of our fathers, the liberty we enjoy—the liberty of free labor on a free soil. We have, therefore, been accustomed to regard with veneration and gratitude the founders of the great republic in which the liberties of the Anglo-Saxon race have been widened beyond all the precedents of the old world, and in which there was nothing to condemn or to lament but the slavery and degradation of men guilty only of a colored skin or an African parentage. We have looked with admiration and sympathy upon the brave, generous and untiring efforts of a large party in the Northern States to deliver the Union from this curse and shame. We rejoiced, sir, in your election to the Presidency, as a splendid proof that the principles of universal freedom and equality were rising to the ascendant. We regarded with abhorrence the conspiracy and rebellion by which it was sought at once to overthrow the supremacy of a government based upon the most popular suffrage in the world, and to perpetuate the hateful inequalities of race. We have ever heard with indignation the slander that ascribed to England sympathy with a rebellion of slaveholders, and all proposals to recognize in friendship a confederacy that boasts of slavery as its cornerstone. We have watched with the warmest interest the steady advance of your policy along the path of emancipation; and on this eve of the day on which your proclamation of freedom takes effect, we pray God to strengthen your hands, to confirm your noble purpose, and to hasten the restoration of that lawful authority which engages, in peace or war, by compensation or by force of arms, to realize the glorious principle on which your constitution is founded—the brotherhood, freedom, and equality of all men."*

On the same day when the workingmen of London in mass meeting assembled framed the above address, the workingmen of Manchester held a meeting for the same purpose. No less than 6,000 persons were present in the hall, the

---

* *Senate Documents.* Washington, 1863.

largest of the city.   The address adopted here
was sent by the Mayor of Manchester by special
messenger to the American Minister at London,
Charles Francis Adams.   The importance which
the American Minister attached to this manifestation of the workingmen may be gathered from
the letter with which he forwarded the address
to Secretary of State Seward, in Washington.
This letter declared:

"This meeting is in every respect a most re-
markable indication of the state of popular sentiment in Great Britain.   It will doubtless make
a strong impression elsewhere, and, if duly followed up, may have the effect of restoring, in a
degree, the amicable feeling between the two
countries."*

The address, whose significance was truly set
forth by this letter of the minister, read as
follows:

"Address from the Workingmen of Manchester
        to His Excellency,
"Abraham Lincoln, President of the United
        States of America.

"As citizens of Manchester, assembled at the
Free Trade Hall, we beg to express our fraternal
sentiments towards you and your country.

"We rejoice in your greatness, as an outgrowth
of England, whose blood and language you share,
whose orderly and legal freedom you have ap-

* *Senate Documents.*   Washington, 1863.

plied to new circumstances, over a region immeasurably greater than our own. We honor your free States as a singularly happy abode for the working millions where industry is honored. One thing alone has, in the past, lessened our sympathy with your country and our confidence in it; we mean the ascendancy of politicians who not merely maintained Negro slavery, but desired to extend and root it more deeply. Since we have discerned, however, that the victory of the free North in the war which has so sorely distressed us as well as afflicted you, will shake off the fetters of the slave, you have attracted our warm and earnest sympathy.

"We joyfully honor you, as the President, and the Congress with you, for the many decisive steps towards practically exemplifying your belief in the words of your great founders: 'All men are created free and equal.'

"You have procured the liberation of the slaves in the district around Washington, and thereby made the centre of your federation visibly free. You have enforced the laws against the slave trade and kept up your fleet against it, even while every ship was wanted for service in your terrible war. You have nobly decided to receive ambassadors from the Negro republics of Hayti and Liberia, thus forever removing that unworthy prejudice which refuses the rights of humanity to men and women on account of their

color. In order more effectually to stop the slave
trade, you have made with our Queen a treaty,
which your Senate has ratified, for the right of
mutual search. Your Congress has decreed freedom as the law forever in the vast unoccupied
or half-settled territories which are directly subject to its legislative power. It has offered pe-
cuniary aid to all the States which will enact
emancipation locally, and has forbidden your
generals to restore fugitive slaves who seek their
protection. You have entreated the slave masters to accept these moderate offers; and, after
long and patient waiting, you, as commander-in-
chief of the army, have appointed to-morrow, the
first of January, 1863, as the day of unconditional
freedom for the slaves of the rebel States.
Heartily do we congratulate you and your country on this humane and righteous course.

"We assume that you cannot now stop short
of a complete uprooting of slavery. It would not
become us to dictate any details, but there are
broad principles of humanity which must guide
you. If complete emancipation in some States be
deferred, though only to a predetermined day,
still, in the interval, human beings should not be
counted chattels. Women must have rights of
chastity and maternity, men the rights of hus-
bands; masters the liberty of manumission. Justice demands for the black, no less than for the
white, the protection of the law—that his voice

may be heard in your courts. Nor must any such abomination be tolerated as slave-breeding States and a slave market—if you are to earn the high reward of all your sacrifices in the approval of the universal brotherhood and of the Divine Father. It is for your free country to decide whether anything but immediate and total emancipation can secure the most indispensable rights of humanity, against the inveterate wickedness of local laws and local executives.

"We implore you, for your own honor and welfare, not to faint in your providential mission. While your enthusiasm is aflame, and the tide of events runs high, let the work be finished effectually. Leave no root of bitterness to spring up and work fresh misery to your children. It is a mighty task, indeed, to reorganize the industry, not only of four millions of the colored race, but of five millions of whites. Nevertheless, the vast progress you have made in the short space of twenty months fills us with hope that every stain on your freedom will shortly be removed, and that the erasure of that foul blot upon civilization and Christianity—chattel slavery—during your Presidency, will cause the name of Abraham Lincoln to be honored and revered by posterity. We are certain that such a glorious consummation will cement Great Britain to the United States in close and enduring regards. Our interests, moreover, are identified with yours.

We are truly one people, though locally separate. And if you have any ill wishers here, be assured that they are chiefly those who oppose liberty at home, and that they will be powerless to stir up quarrels between us, from the very day in which your country becomes, undeniably and without exception, the home of the free.

"Accept our high admiration of your firmness in upholding the proclamation of freedom."

On February 2, 1863, Lincoln sent the following letter in answer to the address of the London workingmen:

"To the workingmen of London: I have received the New Year's address which you have sent me, with a sincere appreciation of the exalted and humane sentiments by which it was inspired.

"As these sentiments are manifestly the enduring support of the free institutions of England, so I am sure also that they constitute the only reliable basis for free institutions throughout the world.

"The resources, advantages and powers of the American people are very great, and they have consequently succeeded to equally great responsibilities. It seems to have developed upon them to test whether a government established on the principles of human freedom can be maintained against an effort to build one upon the exclusive foundation of human bondage. They will rejoice with me in the new evidences which your proceedings furnish that the magnanimity they are exhibiting is justly estimated by the true friends of freedom and humanity in foreign countries.

"Accept my best wishes for your individual welfare, and for the welfare and happiness of the whole British people."

"Abraham Lincoln."*

Previous to this, on January 19th, President Lincoln had sent a more comprehensive reply to the address of the workingmen of Manchester. This reply read as follows:

"Washington, January 19, 1863.
"To the Workingmen of Manchester, England:

"I have the honor to acknowledge the receipt of the address and resolutions which you sent me on the eve of the new year. When I came, on the 4th of March, 1861, through a free and constitutional election to preside in the Government of the United States, the country was found at the verge of civil war. Whatever might have been the cause or whose ever the fault, one duty, paramount to all others, was before me, namely, to maintain and preserve at once the Constitution and the integrity of the Federal Republic. A conscientious purpose to perform this duty is the key to all the measures of administration which have been and to all which will hereafter be pursued.

---

* *Senate Documents.* Third Session, 37th Congress, 1862-1863.

Under our frame of Government and my official
oath, I could not depart from this purpose if I
would. It is not always in the power of government to enlarge or restrict the scope of moral results which follow the policies that they may
deem it necessary for the public safety from time
to time to adopt. I have understood well that
the duty of self-preservation rests solely with the
American people; but I have at the same time
been aware that favor or disfavor of foreign nations might have a material influence in enlarging
or prolonging the struggle with disloyal men in
which the country is engaged. A fair examina-
tion of history has served to authorize a belief
that the past actions and influences of the United
States were generally regarded as having been
beneficial toward mankind. I have, therefore,
reckoned upon the forbearance of nations. Circumstances to which you kindly allude induce me
especially to expect that if justice and good faith
should be practised by the United States, they
would encounter no hostile influence on the part
of Great Britain. It is now a pleasant duty to
acknowledge the demonstration you have given
of your desire that a spirit of amity and peace
toward this country may prevail in the councils
of your Queen, who is respected and esteemed in
your own country only more than she is by the
kindred nation which has its home on this side
of the Atlantic. I know and deeply deplore the

sufferings which the workingmen at Manchester, and in all Europe, are called to endure in this crisis. It has been often and studiously represented that the attempt to overthrow this Government, which was built upon the foundation of human rights, and to substitute for it one which should rest exclusively on the basis of human slavery, was likely to obtain the favor of Europe. Through the action of our disloyal citizens, the workingmen of Europe have been subjected to severe trials, for the purpose of forcing their sanction to that attempt. Under the circumstances, I cannot but regard your decisive utterances upon the question as an instance of sublime Christian heroism which has not been surpassed in any age or in any country. It is indeed an energetic and reinspiring assurance of the inherent power of truth, and of the ultimate and universal triumph of justice, humanity and freedom. I do not doubt that the sentiments you have expressed will be sustained by your great nation; and, on the other hand, I have no hesitation in assuring you that they will excite admiration, esteem and the most reciprocal feelings of friendship among the American people. I hail this interchange of sentiment, therefore, as an augury that whatever else may happen, whatever misfortune may befall your country or my own, the peace and friendship which now exist between the two nations will be, as it shall be my desire to make them, perpetual.

"Abraham Lincoln."*

On the 26th of February the Senate adopted a resolution† requesting that the correspondence between President Lincoln and the workingmen of England be laid before it. This was done, and on March 2d the Senate ordered it sent to the printer and incorporated in the Senate Documents.**

President Lincoln's letter to the workingmen of Manchester recognizes the sacrifices which the workingmen of England made in behalf of the Union, and mentions the sublime heroism shown by them, "unsurpassed in any age or land." The polite phrases in regard to the persons at the head of the English Government were probably inserted for diplomatic reasons. It was really the English working class *alone* that merited the gratitude of the Union.

3. LINCOLN'S ATTITUDE TOWARDS THE WORKING CLASS.

Next to Washington, of all the Presidents, Lincoln ranks highest in the esteem of the American people. It is not only his relation to Negro

---

* *Senate Documents.*   1863.
† *Congressional Globe.* February 26. 1863.
** *Senate Documents.*   Third Session, 37th Congress, 1862-63.

emancipation and his tragic death that have made him the national hero of his country. Mythical tradition also has so glorified him that he is now celebrated for views which he did not hold.

Mythical tradition has especially transfigured Lincoln's attitude towards the working class. He has been credited with prophetic expressions favoring the inference that he foresaw the dominion of capitalist corporations and entertained the fear that all wealth would become concentrated in a few hands, to the great peril of the Republic. Utterances have been ascribed to him counselling the working class to guard well the political rights which they possess and not to allow such rights to be wrested from them. He is even said to have had the economic wisdom to declare that every government should strive to secure for every workingman, as far as possible, the entire product of his labor. In short, Lincoln was represented as a man who had excogitated for himself a clear view of the economic evolution of society, alike in the present and the future, who distinctly recognized the part which the working class would play in this evolution, whose sympathies were entirely with the working class, and who raised a warning voice against the "money power."

Lincoln did not possess this knowledge of economic evolution; he had no idea of the historic part the working class is called to play; he had no idea even of the special significance of the labor movement, and his sympathies were not with the workingmen, in so far as they voiced the demands of a separate class. Lincoln has been extolled as a friend of the workingmen, as almost a Socialist, the Socialist press of the United States even joining in the chorus of praise. This praise has been possible only because sentiments have been ascribed to him which he never uttered, and because certain expressions used by him have been distorted or falsified into their direct opposite.*

Apart from his sentiments in regard to slavery, there are but few among Lincoln's numerous spoken and written utterances which deal with the labor question. In none of these utterances did he declare himself in favor of the working

---

* An ingenious fabrication of utterances on labor purporting to be Lincoln's has been printed and circulated by the thousand in every part of the United States. It consists of five paragraphs, the last four of which are more or less genuine, but are distorted out of their meaning. The first paragraph begins, "I see in the near future a crisis approaching that unnerves me." The whole fabrication was analyzed by W. J. Ghent in *Collier's Weekly* for April 1, 1905. Of the first paragraph Mr. Ghent writes:

"[It] is almost certainly a forgery. The style is not Lincoln's, nor in so far as any one can now say, are the sentiments. Nowhere among his authenticated utterances is there to be found anything resembling either the form or the substance of this paragraph. No one has ever been able to show the original in Lincoln's hand, and repeated demands for its production have met only vague assertions of its existence in some other and generally remote place."

class and its special demands as antagonistic to the other classes of the population. On the contrary, he always avoided recognizing such antagonisms. At Cincinnati, on February 12, 1861, he addressed a meeting of German workingmen. When the chairman declared it as the sense of those present that the working class must be the foundation of all government, Lincoln cautiously remarked:

"I agree with you, Mr. Chairman, that the workingmen are the basis of all government, for the plain reason that they are the more numerous, and as you added, that those were the sentiments of the gentlemen present, representing not only the working class, but citizens of other callings than those of the mechanic, I am happy to concur with you in these sentiments."

Even before this, in March, 1860, Lincoln had expressed himself in regard to the labor movement. The campaign had taken him to New England, where the struggles of the workingmen presented themselves to him more forcibly than elsewhere. In Massachusetts there was in progress a strike of the shoemakers which Senator Douglas had represented as a consequence "of this unfortunate sectional warfare" between the North and the South. In a speech at Hartford, Conn., on March 5, 1860, Lincoln challenged the ridiculous statement of Douglas, saying he "thanked God that we have a system of labor where there can be a strike. Whatever the pressure, there is a point where the workingman may stop." Here, too, Lincoln added cautiously that he did not pretend to be familiar with the subject of the shoe strike. "If you give up your convictions and call slavery right, as they do, you let slavery in upon you—instead of white laborers who can strike, you'll soon have black laborers who can't strike."*

In a speech at New Haven, Conn., on the following day, Lincoln returned to the subject, saying:

"I am glad to see that a system of labor prevails in New England under which laborers can strike when they want to, where they are not obliged to work under all circumstances, and are not tied down and obliged to labor whether you pay them or not. I like the system which lets a man quit when he wants to, and wish it might prevail everywhere. One of the reasons why I am opposed to slavery is just here. What is the true condition of the laborer? I take it that it is the best for all to leave each man free to acquire property as fast as he can. Some will get wealthy. I don't believe in a law to prevent a man from getting rich; it would do more harm than good. So while we do not propose any war upon capital, we do wish to allow the humblest man an equal chance to get rich with everybody

*J. G. Nicolay and J. Hay: *Abraham Lincoln*, I., pp. 615-616.

else. When one starts poor, as most do in the race of life, free society is such that he knows he can better his condition,—he knows that there is no fixed condition of labor for his whole life. I am not ashamed to confess that twenty-five years ago I was a hired laborer, mauling rails, at work on a flatboat—just what might happen to any poor man's son. I want every man to have his chance—and I believe a black man is entitled to it—in which he can better his condition —when he may look forward and hope to be a hired laborer this year and the next, work for himself afterward, and finally to hire men to work for him. That is the true system."*

One may gather from this speech that Lincoln regarded the strike as a rightful weapon in the struggles of the workingmen, but the cautious reserve with which he discusses the matter leaves uncertain his attitude towards labor organizations and particularly towards trade unions.

The two speeches merely show that Lincoln preferred the system of "free labor" to the system of slave labor. For the rest, it is to be seen from his observations that he had no comprehension of the aims and ends of the labor movement or of the special interests of the working class. The labor movement was to him a phenomenon for which he had no understanding and

---

* Nicolay and Hay, I., pp. 625-626.

to which he probably never paid any particular attention.

After his election to the Presidency, Lincoln discussed the question of capital and labor more thoroughly in his message to Congress of December, 1861. He took the same position in this document which he had set forth in his speeches in Hartford and New Haven, and even earlier in an address at Milwaukee, and defended it in almost the same language. This message precisely defined Lincoln's position in relation to economic questions, and it must never be left out of consideration if one wishes to form a true view of the opinions of the man in regard to these matters.

Later, in the year preceding his death, Lincoln made special reference to the propositions in this message, as to a sort of programme to be submitted to workingmen for their consideration, thereby making it plain that he never discarded the views there laid down.

In New York, in 1863, a workingmen's organization had been formed under the name of the Republican Workingmen's Association of New York. This association resolved to make President Lincoln an honorary member. A committee was appointed and sent to Washington for the purpose of apprising the President of his election to an honorary membership in the association and of submitting to him an address. Lincoln received this committee on March 21, 1864, and addressed them as follows:

"Gentlemen of the Committee: The honorary membership in your association, as generously tendered, is gratefully accepted.

"You comprehend, as your address shows, that the existing rebellion means more, and tends to more, than the perpetuation of African slavery—that it is, in fact, a war upon the rights of all working people. Partly to show that this view has not escaped my attention, and partly that I cannot better express myself, I read a passage from the message to Congress in December, 1861:

"'It continues to develop that the insurrection is largely, if not exclusively, a war upon the first principle of popular government—the rights of the people. Conclusive evidence of this is found in the most grave and maturely considered public documents as well as in the general tone of the insurgents. In those documents we find the abridgement of the existing right of suffrage, and the denial to the people of all right to participate in the selection of public officers, except the legislative, boldly advocated, with labored arguments to prove that large control of the people in government is the source of all political evil. Monarchy itself is sometimes hinted at as a possible refuge from the power of the people.

"'In my present position I could scarcely be

justified were I to omit raising a warning voice against this approach of returning despotism.

" 'It is not needed, nor fitting here, that a general argument should be made in favor of popular institutions; but there is one point, with its connections, not so hackneyed as most others, to which I ask a brief attention. It is the effort, to place *capital* on an equal footing with, if not above, *labor*, in the structure of government. It is assumed that labor is available only in connection with capital, that nobody labors unless somebody else, owning capital, somehow by the use of it induces him to labor. This assumed, it is next considered whether it is best, that capital shall *hire* laborers and thus induce them to work by their own consent, or *buy* them and drive them to it without their consent. Having proceeded so far, it is naturally concluded that all laborers are either *hired* laborers or what we call slaves, and, further, it is assumed that whoever is once a hired laborer, is fixed in that condition for life.

" 'Now, there is no such relation between capital and labor as assumed; nor is there any such thing as a free man being fixed for life in the condition of a hired laborer. Both these assumptions are false, and all inferences from them are groundless.

" 'Labor is prior to, and independent of, capital. Capital is only the fruit of labor and could never have existed if labor had not first existed.

Labor is the superior of capital, and deserves much the higher consideration. Capital has its rights, which are as worthy of protection as any other rights. Nor is it denied that there is, and probably always will be, a relation between capital and labor, producing mutual benefits. The error is in assuming that the whole labor of the community exists within that relation. A few men own capital, and that few avoid labor themselves, and, with their capital, hire or buy another few to labor for them. A large majority belong to neither class—neither work for others, nor have others working for them. In most of the Southern States a majority of the whole people, of all colors, are neither slaves nor masters; while in the Northern, a large majority are neither hirers nor hired. Men with their families—wives, sons, and daughters—work for themselves, on their farms, in their houses, and in their shops, taking the whole product to themselves, and asking no favors of capital on the one hand, nor of hired laborers or slaves on the other. It is not forgotten that a considerable number of persons mingle their own labor with capital, that is: they labor with their own hands, and also buy or hire others to labor for them, but this is only a mixed and not a distinct class. No principle stated is disturbed by the existence of the mixed class.

" 'Again, as has already been said, there is not, of necessity, any such thing as the free hired laborer being fixed to that condition for life. Many independent men everywhere in those States, a few years back in their lives, were hired laborers. The prudent penniless beginner in the world labors for wages a while, saves a surplus with which to buy tools or land for himself, then labors on his own account another while, and at length hires another new beginner to help him. This is the just and generous and prosperous system, which opens the way to all—gives hope to all and consequent energy and progress and improvement of condition to all. No men living are more worthy to be trusted than those who toil up from poverty—none less inclined to take or touch that which they have not honestly earned. Let them beware of surrendering a political power which they already possess, and which, if surrendered, will surely be used to close the door of advancement against such as they, and to fix new disabilities and burdens upon them, till all of liberty shall be lost.'

"The views then expressed remain unchanged, nor have I much to add. None are so deeply interested to resist the present rebellion as the working people. Let them beware of prejudice, working division and hostility among themselves. The most notable feature of a disturbance in your city last summer was the hanging of some working people by other working people. It should never be so. The strongest bond of human sympathy, outside of the family relation, should be one uniting all working people, of all nations, and tongues, and kindreds. Nor should this lead to a war upon property, or the owners of property. Property is the fruit of labor; property is desirable; is a positive good in the world. That some should be rich shows that others may become rich, and hence is just encouragement to industry and enterprise. Let not him who is houseless pull down the house of another, but let him work diligently and build one for himself, thus by example assuring that his own shall be safe from violence when built."*

It is evident from this address that Lincoln considered himself as belonging to the lower middle class (petty bourgeoisie) and that he was imbued by its ideals. Nothing is more natural, considering the state of social evolution in America at that time and Lincoln's individual development. Lincoln denies the existence of an industrial proletariat, "fixed to that condition for life." In the light of his lower middle-class experiences and ideals he still saw for every one the possibility of advancement from wage worker to proprietor. His observations are a glorification of the lower middle class, the men who are neither capitalists nor wage-workers. The former wage worker who advances by his own efforts and then hires another beginner as a wage

---

* Nicolay and Hay, pp. 501-502.

worker, thus becoming a small employer—such
is Lincoln's ideal. That is to him "the just and
generous and prosperous system." He warns this
stratum of the population, who "toil up from
poverty," to beware of surrendering their political rights and their political power. It is not the
working men whom Lincoln counsels to vigilance
over their political rights, but the lower middle
class. And whoever might still entertain the
slightest doubt concerning Lincoln's position
among the classes constituting society, and the
distance by which he was still separated from
the Socialist point of view, will be set right by
the close of his address to the New York labor
committee, by his glorification of property and
its owners, and by his warning to workingmen not
to "make war upon property." If he was at all
aware of Socialist views and had formed an
opinion concerning them, it must have been a
hostile one. This was quite natural! The labor
question and its implications were foreign to him.
He represented the farmer and the lower middle
class with whom his strength lay, and who at that
period constituted the most powerful stratum of
the population of the Northern States of the
Union.

The passage in Lincoln's address to the New
York labor committee, "the strongest bond of
human sympathy, outside of the family relation, should be one uniting all working people, of

all nations and tongues and kindreds," has led some to conclude that its author must have had an understanding of the international solidarity of the working class and of the special class solidarity which is peculiar to the labor movement on a higher plane. It is possible that the heroic attitude in favor of the Union assumed by the working class of England during the war had awakened in him a slight understanding of the class solidarity of workingmen, but it is not probable, and we must consider that beautiful passage as a mere mode of expression without any deeper significance. If one were to draw inferences from a single passage of this kind as to Lincoln's general way of thinking in regard to the labor movement, one would have to concede the right of other classes to derive precisely contrary conclusions from his remarks in the speech at New Haven: "I take it that it is the best for all to leave each man free to acquire property as fast as he can," and "I don't believe in a law to prevent a man from getting rich."

But there is still another document on the strength of which a claim has been made for Lincoln's approach to Socialism. In 1847 Lincoln had outlined a speech on the protective tariff and free trade which he intended to deliver in Congress. In this outline occur the following statements:

"In the early days of our race the Almighty said

to the first of our race, 'In the sweat of thy face shalt thou eat bread,' and since then, if we except the light and the air of heaven, no good thing has been or can be enjoyed by us without having first cost labor. And inasmuch as most good things are produced by labor, it follows that all such things of right belong to those whose labor has produced them. But it has so happened, in all ages of the world, that some have labored, and others have without labor enjoyed a large proportion of the fruits. This is wrong, and should not continue. To secure to each laborer the whole product of his labor, or as nearly as possible, is a worthy object of any good government.

"But then the question arises, how can a government best effect this? In our own country, in its present condition, will the protective principle advance or retard this object? Upon this subject the habits of our whole species fall into three great classes—useful labor, useless labor and idleness. Of these, the first only is meritorious, and to it all the products of labor rightfully belong; but the two latter, while they exist, are heavy pensioners upon the first, robbing it of a large portion of its just rights. The only remedy for this is to, so far as possible, drive useless labor and idleness out of existence. And, first, as to useless labor. Before making war upon this we must learn to distinguish it from useful. It appears to me that all labor done directly and indirectly in carrying articles to the place of consumption, which could have been produced in sufficient abundance, with as little labor, at the place of consumption as at the place they were carried from, is useless labor."*

On the basis of these considerations Lincoln attempted to demonstrate that it would be useful labor to inaugurate and develop in the South, where cotton is indigenous, the cotton spinning and weaving industry. To this end he demanded the maintenance of the protective tariff.

He writes literally:

"I try to show that the abandonment of the protective policy by the American Government must result in the increase of both useless labor and idleness, and so, in proportion, must produce want and ruin among the people."

Considered out of their context, Lincoln's introductory remarks in this outline might produce the impression that he indeed inclined towards certain Socialist views according to which the product of labor should belong to him who created it. It is even not impossible that Lincoln, at the high tide of the Fourierist movement, at the time when he wrote his outline, had become acquainted with newspapers and pamphlets containing similar propositions and that he drew his

---

* Nicolay and Hay, I., p. 92 ff.

inspiration from these. It is certain that he was
a reader of Greeley's *Tribune*. But in the connection where we find it, the sentence "to secure
to each laborer the whole product of his labor,
or as nearly as possible, is a worthy object of
any good government," cannot mean that the
wage worker is to receive the product of his
labor. That labor alone produces values was by
no means clear to Lincoln. In his view the manufacturer who exploited a number of men was
also doing useful work, and he, too, was therefore entitled to the product of his labor. The
transport of merchandise he did not consider as
useful labor, and the workingmen engaged in the
transportation of merchandise were therefore not
entitled to a share of the product. Lincoln's So-
cialist-sounding phrases of 1847 by no means
bore a Socialist meaning, they could not bear
such a meaning, because their author had no conception of the working class as a well-defined
stratum of the population, with economic interests of its own and with definite historical aims.

Abraham Lincoln was not a Socialist, nor was
he particularly friendly to workingmen as the
components of a class. The ideas of the modern
working-class movement were to him foreign
ideas and remained so even in his later years. He
stood on the ground of the lower middle class
and the farmer element, to which he himself be-

longed. He was a man of his age, with whose ideas he was imbued. He was not a man of the future, and he knew nothing of the ideas of the future. And the ideas which have been developed by the labor movement were to him the ideas of a future time.

CHAPTER VI.

THE INTERNATIONAL WORKINGMEN'S ASSOCIATION AND THE AMERICAN CIVIL WAR.

1. ADDRESS OF THE GENERAL COUNCIL TO ABRAHAM LINCOLN.

On September 28, 1864, in St. Martin's Hall in London, there took place that famous meeting of workingmen which gave birth to the International Workingmen's Association, an organization which powerfully stimulated and promoted the labor movement of all countries in the sixties. This meeting appointed a provisional central committee for the management of the affairs of the new organization, which came later to be called the General Council, and which was composed of representatives of different nationalities.

Even before the foundation of the International Workingmen's Association, it was above all others the men who became the members of the General Council who had worked for the cause of the American North in their circles, and who had encouraged and inspired the English working class in their heroic stand against the manufacturers and the Government.

On November 27, 1864, Karl Marx, the leading spirit of the General Council, wrote thus about the elements composing this committee to his friend Joseph Weydemeyer, then in the United States:

"Its English members are mostly chiefs of the local trades unions, hence the real labor kings of London, the same people who gave Garibaldi such a rousing welcome, and who by their monster meeting in St. James' Hall (Bright in the chair) prevented Palmerston from declaring war against the United States when he was on the point of doing it."*

Previous to the organization of the International Workingmen's Association Marx also had thrown his influence to the leaders of the English workingmen in favor of the Union cause.

The General Council of the International continued the agitation in this direction which its members had previously begun.

In the beginning of November, 1864, Lincoln was elected for the second time to the Presidency of the United States. Under the direct influence and upon the suggestion of the General Council of the International Workingmen's Association, the workingmen of London arranged a new series of meetings to protest against the anti-Union attitude of the manufacturers and the Government

---

* F. Mehring, *Neue Beiträge zur Biographie von K. Marx und F. Engels, Neue Zeit,* 1906-07, Vol. II, p. 224.

of their country.   It was Marx who furnished the initiative for this renewal of agitation.*

In one of the following meetings of the General Council, one of its members, Dick, made a motion, which was seconded by G. Howell, to draft an address to the American people congratulating them upon their struggles and sacrifices in behalf of the principles of freedom and upon their re-election of Lincoln to the Presidency of the United States.   A committee was appointed to formulate this address, and this committee submitted its draft, the author of which was Marx, to the General Council at its meeting on November 29th.   The draft was accepted, and a resolution was adopted to forward it by a committee to Charles Francis Adams, the American Minister at London, for transmission to his Government.   The following is the text of the address:

"To Abraham Lincoln, President of the United States of America.

"Sir:—We congratulate the American people upon your re-election by a large majority.   If resistance to the Slave Power was the watchword of your first election, the triumphal war-cry of your re-election is Death to Slavery.

"From the commencement of the titanic Amer-

---

* According to letters to the author by Friedrich Lessner, of London, at the time a member of the General Council of the International Workingmen's Association.

ican strife the workingmen of Europe felt distinctively that the Star Spangled Banner carried the destiny of their class. The contest for the territories which opened the *dire epopèe*, was it not to decide whether the virgin soil of immense tracts should be wedded to the labor of the immigrant or be prostituted by the tramp of the slave-driver?

"When an oligarchy of 300,000 slaveholders dared to inscribe for the first time in the annals of the world 'Slavery' on the banner of armed revolt, when on the very spots where hardly a century ago the idea of one great Democratic Republic had first sprung up, whence the first declaration of the Rights of Man was issued, and the first impulse given to the European Revolution of the eighteenth century, when on those very spots counter-revolution, with systematic thoroughness, gloried in rescinding 'the ideas entertained at the time of the formation of the old constitution' and maintained 'slavery to be a beneficial institution,' indeed, the only solution of the great problem of the 'relation of capital to labor,' and cynically proclaimed property in man 'the cornerstone of the new edifice,'—then the working classes of Europe understood at once, even before the fanatic partisanship of the upper classes, for the Confederate gentry had given its dismal warning, that the slaveholders' rebellion was to sound the tocsin for a general holy war

cf property against labor, and that for the men
of labor, with their hopes for the future, even
their past conquests were at stake in that tremendous conflict on the other side of the Atlantic.
Everywhere they bore therefore patiently the
hardships imposed upon them by the cotton crisis,
opposed enthusiastically the pro-slavery intervention—importunities of their betters—and from
most parts of Europe contributed their quota of
blood to the good of the cause.

"While the workingmen, the true political
power of the North, allowed slavery to defile their
own republic, while before the Negro, mastered
and sold without his concurrence, they boasted
it the highest prerogative of the white-skinned
laborer to sell himself and choose his own master,
they were unable to attain the true freedom of
labor, or to support their European brethren in
their struggle for emancipation; but this barrier
to progress has been swept off by the red sea of
civil war.

"The workingmen of Europe felt sure that,
as the American War of Independence initiated
a new era of ascendency for the middle class, so
the American Anti-slavery War will do for the
working classes. They consider it an earnest sign
of the epoch to come that it fell to the lot of
Abraham Lincoln, the single-minded son of the
working class, to lead his country through the

matchless struggle for the rescue of the enchained race and the reconstruction of a social world.

"Signed on behalf of the International Workingmen's Association, the Central Council:

"Longmaid, Worley, Whitlock, Blackmore, Hartwell, Pidgeon, Lucraft, Weston, Dell, Nicars, Shaw, Lake, Buckley, Osborn, Howell, Carter, Wheeler, Starnsby, Morgan, Grossmith, Dick, Denoual, Jourdain, Morissot, Leroux, Bordage, Bosquet, Talandier, Dupont, L. Wolf, Aldrovandi, Lama, Solustri, Nuspert, Eccarius, Wolf, Lessner, Pfänder, Lochner, Taub, Balliter, Rypcrynski, Hansen, Schantzenbeck, Smales, Cornelius, Peterson, Otto, Bagnagatti, Setocri; George Odgers, President of the Council; P. V. Lubez, Corresponding Secretary for France; Karl Marx, Corresponding Secretary for Germany; C. P. Fontana, Corresponding Secretary for Italy; J. E. Holtorp, Corresponding Secretary for Poland; H. F. Jung, Corresponding Secretary for Switzerland; William Cremer, Hon. General Secretary, 18 Greek Street, Soho, London W." *

At the meeting of the General Council on Tuesday, February 2, 1865, the General Secretary read a reply, written by the United States Minister in London, which was as follows:

---

* *Beehive.* London, Jan. 7, 1865.

"Legation of the United States of America.

"London, Jan. 28, 1865.

"Sir:—I am directed to inform you that the address of the Central Council of your Association, which was duly transmitted through this legation to the President of the United States of America, has been received by him. So far as the sentiments expressed by it are personal, they are accepted by him with a sincere and anxious desire that he may be able to prove himself not unworthy of the confidence which has been recently extended to him by his fellow-citizens, and by so many friends of humanity and progress throughout the world. The Government of the United States of America has a clear consciousness that its policy neither is, nor could be, reactionary; but at the same time it adheres to the course which it adopted at the beginning of abstaining everywhere from propagandism and unlawful intervention. It strives to do equal justice to all states and to all men, and it relies upon the beneficent results of that effort for support at home. and for respect and good will throughout the world. Nations do not exist for themselves alone, but to promote the welfare and happiness of mankind by benevolent intercourse and example. It is in this relation that the United States regard their cause in the present conflict with slavery-maintaining insurgents as the cause of human nature, and they derive new encouragement to persevere from the testimony of the workingmen of Europe that the National Alliance is favored with the enlightened approval and earnest sympathies.

"I have the honor to be, Sir,
"Your obedient servant,
"Charles Francis Adams."

The attitude of the General Council of the International Workingmen's Association, as reflected in the address to President Lincoln, did not, however, meet with the approval of all its sympathizers in the United States. Among those who protested against it were especially the members of the Communist Club of New York, who held that Lincoln's policy did not deserve to be thus honored.

2. ADDRESS OF THE GENERAL COUNCIL OF THE INTERNATIONAL WORKINGMEN'S ASSOCIATION TO PRESIDENT ANDREW JOHNSON.

On April 14, 1865, Lincoln was fatally wounded in Ford's Theatre in Washington by a shot in the head fired by the actor, John Wilkes Booth. He died the next morning. At the same time Southern fanatics attempted to kill Secretary of State Seward in his bed and dangerously wounded him and his son. Vice-President Johnson succeeded Lincoln as President of the Union.

It was characteristic of the feeling towards the United States in the dominant circles of England that one of their mouthpieces in the press, on the arrival of the news of Lincoln's assassination, should publish the following significant suggestion: "The dagger or the pistol in the hands of the weakest worm that crawls in human shape upon the earth can change the destinies of nations or divert the current opinion into a new channel." And immediately following this sentence, without any transition, the paper described Lincoln's successor, Andrew Johnson, as a "bloodthirsty scoundrel," as the scum and outcast of mankind, as a most dangerous tyrant.*

It was of course only the most rabid element among the English public that extolled the assassin Booth as a champion of liberty, as a worthy successor of Brutus and of Tell, while on the other hand a large portion of those who had hitherto been hostile to Lincoln condemned Booth's deed.

On the report of Lincoln's death, the General Council of the International Workingmen's Association resolved to send another address to America, this time to the successor of the murdered President, Andrew Johnson. The address was adopted May 13th, and read as follows:*

---

* *Der Deutsche Eidgenosse.* London and Hamburg. 1865, p. 42.

* The address was published in the London *Beehive* of May 20, 1865. It has been impossible to procure a copy of this issue of the *Beehive,* and the author of the present treatise has therefore been compelled to retranslate the

"Address of the International Workingmen's Association to President Johnson.

"To Andrew Johnson, President of the United States.

"Dear Sir:

"The demon of the 'peculiar institution,' for whose preservation the South rose in arms, did not permit its devotees to suffer honorable defeat on the open battlefield. What had been conceived in treason, must necessarily end in infamy. As Philip II.'s war in behalf of the Inquisition produced a Gérard, so Jefferson Davis's rebellion a Booth.

"We shall not seek for words of mourning and of horror when the heart of two continents is throbbing with emotion. Even the sycophants who year after year and day after day were busily engaged in morally stabbing Abraham Lincoln and the great republic of which he was the head —even they are dismayed in the presence of this universal outburst of popular feeling and vie with one another in strewing flowers of rhetoric upon his open grave. They have at last come to recognize that he was a man whom defeat could not dishearten, nor success intoxicate, who imperturbably pressed on towards his great goal with-

address into English from a German translation of it to which he has had access. The wording which he here submits is therefore certain not to correspond with the original in every particular, but he feels that he can vouch for the essential accuracy of the message it conveyed.

out ever imperilling it by blind haste, who advanced deliberately and never retraced a step, who was never carried away by popular favor and never discouraged by the subsidence of popular enthusiasm, who answered acts of severity with the sunbeams of a loving heart, who brightened gloomy exhibitions of passion by the smile of humor, and who accomplished his titanic task as simply and as modestly as rulers by divine right are wont to do trifling things with great pomp and circumstance; in a word, he was one of those rare men who succeed in becoming great without ceasing to be good. So great, indeed, was the modesty of this great and good man that the world discovered that he was a hero only when he had died as a martyr.

"To be chosen at the side of such a leader as the second victim by the hellish demons of slavery was an honor of which Mr. Seward was worthy. Was he not in a period of general indecision so perspicacious as to foresee the 'irrepressible conflict' and so unterrified as to foretell it? Did he not in the gloomiest moments of this conflict prove himself true to the duty of the Roman never to despair of the republic and its destiny? We hope with all our heart that he and his son will be, in less than ninety days, restored to health, to public activity, and to the well-deserved honors which await them.

"After a gigantic Civil War which, if we consider its colossal extension and its vast scene of action, seems in comparison with the Hundred Years' War and the Thirty Years' War and the Twenty-three Years' War of the Old World scarcely to have lasted ninety days, the task, Sir, devolves upon you to uproot by law what the sword has felled, and to preside over the more difficult work of political reconstruction and social regeneration. The profound consciousness of your great mission will preserve you from all weakness in the execution of your stern duties. You will never forget that the American people at the inauguration of the new era of the emancipation of labor placed the burden of leadership on the shoulders of two men of labor—Abraham Lincoln the one, and the other Andrew Johnson.

"Signed in the name of the International Workingmen's Association by the General Council, May 13, 1865:

"Charles Kaub, L. Delle, H. Klimrosch, M. Salbasella, Edward Coulson, G. Lochner, I. Weston, G. Howell, F. Lessner, G. Eccarius, H. Bollster, Bordage, C. Pfänder, I. Osborne, B. Luirass, A. Valtien, N. P. Stansen, P. Peterson, I. Buckley, R. Shaw, K. Schapper, A. Janks, P. Fox, I. H. Longmaid, M. Morgan, G. L. Wheeler, I. D. Nicass, L. C. Vorley, Dr. Stainsby, F. Carter. E. Holtorp, Secretary for Poland; K. Marx, Secretary for Germany; H. Jung, Secretary for Switzerland; E. Dupont, Secretary for France;

E. Whitlock, Financial Secretary; G. Odgers, President; W. R. Cremer, General Secretary."

3.   ADDRESS OF THE GENERAL COUNCIL TO THE PEOPLE OF THE UNITED STATES.

In September, 1865, the International met in conference in London, as the first congress of the Association which was to have taken place at this time in Brussels had been made impossible by the action of the Belgian Government. This London conference once more returned to a discussion of the question of slavery and resolved to send an address to the American people. The following was the address:

"Address of the Conference of the International Workingmen's Association of September 25, 1865.

"To the People of the United States of America.

"Citizens of the Great Republic, once more we address you, not in sympathetic condolence, but in words of congratulation.

"Had we not most profoundly sympathized with you in your times of trouble, when foes within and without were eagerly bent on destroying your Government and the principles of universal justice upon which it is based, we should not now venture to congratulate you upon your success.

"But we have never swerved in our loyalty to

your cause, which is the cause of all mankind;
nor did we ever despair of its final triumph, not
even in the darkest shadows of its mishaps.

"In firm devotion to, and unfaltering faith in,
those principles of equality and fraternal com-
munion for which you drew the sword, we were
convinced that as soon as the conflict should be
over and victory won, you would return it to its
scabbard, and peace would once more come to
your country and joy to your people.

"Success has justified our expectations. Your
war is the only example known of a government
fighting against a fraction of its own citizens for
the freedom of the people.

"Above all we congratulate you upon the term-
ination of the war and the preservation of the
Union. The Stars and the Stripes, which your
own sons had brutally trampled in the dust, once
more flutter in the breeze from the Atlantic to
the Pacific Ocean, never again, we trust, to be in-
sulted by your own children and never again to
wave over bloody battlefields, whether those of
domestic insurrection or those of foreign war.

"And may those misguided citizens who dis-
played so much valor on the battlefield in a
wicked cause now display as much zeal in helping
to heal the wounds which they struck and in restoring peace to the common country.

"Again we felicitate you upon the removal of
the cause of these years of affliction—upon the

abolition of slavery. This stain upon your otherwise so shining escutcheon is forever wiped out.
Never again shall the hammer of the auctioneer
announce in your market-places sales of human
flesh and blood and make mankind shudder at the
cruel barbarism.

"Your noblest blood was shed in washing away
these stains, and desolation has spread its black
shroud over your country in penance for the past.

"To-day you are free, purified through your
sufferings. A brighter future is dawning upon
your glorious republic, proclaiming to the old
world that a government of the people and by
the people is a government for the people and not
for a privileged minority.

"We had the honor to express to you our
sympathy in your affliction, to send you a word
of encouragement in your struggles, and to congratulate you upon your success. Permit us to
add a word of counsel for the future.

"Injustice against a fraction of your people
having been followed by such dire consequences,
put an end to it. Declare your fellow citizens
from this day forth free and equal, without any
reserve. If you refuse them citizens' rights while
you exact from them citizens' duties, you will
sooner or later face a new struggle which will
once more drench your country in blood.

"The eyes of Europe and of the whole world
are on your attempts at reconstruction, and foes

are ever ready to sound the death-knell of republican institutions as soon as they see their
opportunity.

"We therefore admonish you, as brothers in
a common cause, to sunder all the chains of freedom, and your victory will be complete."

The policy of conciliation initiated by the
American Government in regard to the South,
and the adoption of the constitutional amend-
ments affirming the political equality of the Negroes, were steps in accordance with the address which the conference of the International
Workingmen's Association directed to the people
of the United States.

CHAPTER VII.

THE LABOR MOVEMENT DURING THE CIVIL WAR.

1. The Draft Riot in New York.

As we have seen, the outbreak of the Civil War had the immediate effect of destroying the labor movement in the United States. But what it had destroyed, it soon called to life again. The rise in the price of all food products, the coincident lowering of the workingmen's standard of life, the scarcity of labor, the rapid development of industry and capitalism accompanying the war, furnished so many factors favorable to a revival and rapid rise of the labor movement. For the war and everything connected with it roused the class consciousness of the American workingmen and the feeling of class division in society to a degree unequalled in the later history of the American labor movement.

The revival of the labor movement during the war, and the intensified struggle of the workingmen for the betterment of their lot, challenged the opposition of the capitalists, who resisted with all their might the demand of the workingmen for shorter hours and for an increase in their wages to meet the enhanced prices of their necessities. While the Northern armies, largely recruited from among the wage earners all over the country, were waging the war that was destined to abolish Negro slavery, and while the Northern capitalists were enriching themselves at the expense of this war, the latter on their part were conducting a campaign in the North against the white workingmen in an endeavor to force them into an economic condition which, from a purely economic point of view, did not materially differ from the condition of the Negroes in the South. It was the capitalists' aim during the war against black slavery to fortify, by all possible means, white slavery.

To achieve this end, they undertook to destroy the trade unions which the workingmen had organized. They sought to do this partly through their economic power, partly by passing laws against labor organizations in the legislatures, and partly, also, as we shall see, by availing themselves of the forces which had been called to arms for the destruction of Negro slavery and the preservation of the Union, for the purpose of fortifying wage slavery and turning these forces against the workingmen and their unions.

The class antagonisms between capitalists and workingmen during the war found expression not only in the direct struggles for higher wages and shorter hours, but they manifested themselves on all other occasions. As is always the case, the ruling class, through the legislatures, sought to unload all burdens from their own shoulders upon those of the great mass of the people. This was true not only in regard to the financial burdens, but also in regard to the burdens of blood.

Early in the year 1863, when, after hard struggles, the end of the war seemed still far off, and some difficulty was found in securing the necessary volunteers for the army, a law was passed in Congress which authorized the drafting of citizens for the army. The attempted enforcement of this law led to disturbances in the city of New York which cost hundreds of lives and for days provoked bloody encounters between the police and military and the insurgent masses of workingmen. In New York political opponents of the war and secret friends of the slaveholders were especially active. They took the draft as a pretext for inflaming the mass of their followers, consisting principally of Irish unskilled laborers, against the war and later also against the cause of the Union itself. The execution of the draft was entrusted to Federal provosts, an act which was represented by the Democrats as a violation of State rights. The majority of the metropolitan newspapers opposed the enforcement of the draft. When its execution was undertaken, on July 13, 1863, it met everywhere with resistance. Workmen who were engaged in tearing down a building were requested by Federal provosts to give their names for the draft. They refused and drove away the officers by force. The movement spread over the whole city. Everywhere there was a congregation of excited crowds. The mobs visited the workshops and factories and compelled the men to stop work and join them. Prominent police officers were attacked by force and barely escaped with their lives. Offices where the drafting officers were at work were stormed, the lists of names were destroyed, and the houses set on fire. Firemen were forcibly prevented from putting out the flames. Telegraph wires were cut. Incendiarism was followed by plunder. Numerous houses were sacked, street cars and omnibuses ceased running, stores on Broadway, the avenues and throughout the greater portion of the city were closed.

These disturbances, which were at first directed only against the enforcement of the draft, were within a few days turned against the unfortunate Negroes. The cause of the war, and hence of the draft, they incurred the hatred of the masses, and it seems as if there had been a deliberate deflection of the mob's fury against them. The Negroes were disliked by the unskilled workmen of New York, also for the reason that on various occasions they had been employed by the capitalists as strike-breakers in putting down the labor troubles. They had made themselves especially offensive in a strike of the longshoremen in New York harbor, who were mostly Irishmen. The Negroes' dwellings were set on fire, and a number of them were killed. The disturbances assumed a hostile attitude to the Union. Attempts were made to storm the buildings of Abolitionist newspapers, especially the *Tribune,* and the private residence of Horace Greeley. Cheers were heard for Jefferson Davis, the President of the Southern Confederacy.

From the start the police had met the riotous masses with terrible brutality, using their clubs indiscriminately. The rage of the people would certainly not have reached the proportions it did if they had not been so fiendishly treated by the police. In the beginning "the mob simply desired to break up the draft in some of the upper districts of the city and destroy the registers in which certain names were enrolled," according to a contemporary pamphlet* written in praise of the police. But the terrible treatment of the masses, and the frightful bloodshed, first by the police, then by the military summoned from Fort Hamilton, West Point and other outlying garrisons, drove the masses far beyond the original scope of the movement. On the west side barri-

---

* S. F. Headley: *The Great Riots of New York.* 1873.

cades were erected, whereupon the soldiers fired volleys into the crowds and dispersed them by shells. The police ordered to attack the people were told to make no arrests; the military were under like instructions. Whoever came in their way was clubbed or shot down. The soldiers fired so recklessly that they even hit policemen.

The disturbances lasted from Monday until Friday. More than fifty buildings were burned. The loss in property was estimated at $1,200,000. The number of persons killed by the police and the military was variously estimated at from 400 or 500 to 1,200 (Headley). As the bodies of the dead were in most cases removed by their relatives, the exact number could not be ascertained. Eleven Negroes and seven other men were killed by the rioters. Only three policemen came to their death, but many were wounded by stones and other missiles. The enormous difference in the number of killed among the masses and among the armed forces shows what little justification there was for this terrible slaughter in the ranks of the workingmen. How small was the number of prisoners is shown by the fact that only nineteen persons were sentenced by the courts for participation in this riot, which had been accompanied by bloodshed, incendiarism and plunder.

Now the cause of this Draft Riot in New York was exclusively *social*. It arose from the fact that the propertied class, with all the force of its economic and political prestige, attempted to unload the blood-tax which the war demanded from its own shoulders on to those of the working class. The draft law as passed by Congress provided that anyone could secure exemption from military service by the payment of $300. In this way the rich man, to whom this small sum meant nothing, was virtually exempt from military duty, a discrimination between the classes which was deeply resented as an injustice by those who could not raise the money. According to Headley:

"Most of those drawn were laboring men or poor mechanics, who were unable to hire a substitute. . . . . If a well-known name, that of a man of wealth, was among the number, it only increased the exasperation, for the law exempted everyone drawn who would pay three hundred dollars towards a substitute. This was taking practically the whole number of soldiers called for out of the laboring classes. A great proportion of these being Irish, it naturally became an Irish question and eventually an Irish riot."*

The social and class character of the Draft Riot is here most clearly presented. The municipal authorities seem to have recognized this too, although political motives may also have entered into it. On the fourth day of the riot

---

* Headley, p. 149.

it was announced that the draft had been suspended, and the City Council had passed an ordinance appropriating $2,500,000 toward paying $300 exemption money to the poor who might be drafted. But as in the meantime 10,000 soldiers had been concentrated in New York, and the force of the riot had been spent, the process of drafting continued nevertheless.

As already stated, the principal participants in these encounters were Irish workingmen. This fact was due to their affiliation with the Democratic party, which favored slavery. The numerous German workingmen in the city took no part in the disturbances. They rather held themselves aloof, because in the main they sided with the opponents of slavery.

The riots were followed by a number of large mass meetings in New York which, in the name of the working class, protested against the sentiments and expressions hostile to the Union on the part of a fraction of workingmen during the disturbances. It was fortunate for the Union's cause that the majority of the workingmen of New York, in those July days of 1863, did not make common cause with the Irishmen who had been driven to riot and revolt by the injustice done them by the property holders and the legislature. For though the crisis of the war had just been passed by the victories of Gettysburg and Vicksburg, the South was at the time exerting its utmost strength, and the Union was still in a dangerous position. A successful revolt in New York might in those days have been followed by consequences which one trembles to contemplate, especially if the menacing attitude of the foreign powers, and particularly of England, is considered. The Union would have fallen on evil days had not the American and the German workingmen of the city of New York at that time exalted its cause above that of their own class.

2. LAWS AGAINST LABOR ORGANIZATIONS.

It took a long time before the standard of life, which at the outbreak of the Civil War had been lowered by the depreciation of the paper currency and the high prices of the necessaries of life, was again raised by the struggles and the organized efforts of the workingmen. Even in January, 1864, three years after the outbreak of the war, Sylvis referred to the impaired condition of the workingmen incident to the war in the following words:

"Go with me to the magnificent cotton mills of the Eastern States, and I will show you a picture such as you have never seen. A few years ago men received fair wages in these mills, and were able to live comfortably from their earnings, and to raise and educate their children well; but now, by this downward tendency of the price of labor, by this gradual reduction of wages, it requires the combined labor of the husband, wife and every child old enough to walk to the factory, for from twelve to fifteen hours a day, to earn sufficient to keep body and soul together."*

The year 1864 witnessed redoubled efforts on the part of the American working class to regain the position it had occupied previous to the outbreak of the war. New organizations and workingmen's demonstrations of various kinds were daily occurrences. The capitalists of the North, made haughty by the enormous power which had come to them in the last few years, combined to hold down the labor movement and to depress wages to a starvation level. It was the fixed purpose of the capitalists of the country to destroy all labor organizations. One of these capitalists, more honest than the rest, said to Sylvis:

"The day is not far distant when the condition of the workingmen will be far worse than ever before. The day will come when men who are now active in the labor union movement will be forced upon their bended knees to beg for work. . . . . A spirit of retaliation has been aroused in the bosom of every employer, the fruits of which are being manifested in the widespread and universal organization of capitalists

---

* Sylvis, pp. 104-105.

for the avowed and publicly proclaimed purpose of destroying your unions."*

In the youthful exuberance of their class rule the attitude of the capitalists towards their workingmen was so arrogant that even American judges, not yet completely corrupted by capitalism, as in later years, raised their voice in rebuke of it. It was at this time that a certain Judge Tilford, while denouncing an attempt at a reduction of wages, said:

"It cannot and must not be. By the laws of ancient Rome, a convicted traitor was hurled from the Tarpeian Rock. Let the man who, in this crisis, advocates the reduction of wages, 'or the subjugation of labor to the whims and caprices of the wealthy, by denying to labor the right to regulate its own affairs,' be girdled and encircled with burning fagots, and receive the fate of the Roman felon."†

But neither the opposition of the workingmen nor voices from their own ranks, such as that of Judge Tilford, could shake the capitalists in their resolution to destroy the organizations of the workingmen. They were not satisfied with their own activity in this direction, but invoked the assistance of the State. In the spring of 1864 laws were introduced in the Legislatures in New York, Massachusetts and other States,

---

* Sylvis, pp. 132-133.
† Sylvis, p. 131.

termed laws against intimidation, but really so drawn as practically to destroy all trade-union organizations. The bill presented in the New York Assembly read as follows:

"An Act to Punish Unlawful Interference With Employers and Employees.

"The People of the State of New York, represented in the Senate and Assembly, do enact as follows:

"Section I. Any person who shall himself, or in combination with any other person or persons, by force or threats of any kind, either

"1. Prevent or deter, or attempt to prevent or deter, any other person or persons from engaging or continuing in any lawful employment. labor or undertaking, in such manner and upon such terms as he or they may choose or accept;

"2. Prevent or deter, or attempt to prevent or deter, any other person or persons from employing such workmen, laborers or employees that he or they desire to employ, and in such manner and on such terms as he or they may choose or accept, shall be guilty of a misdemeanor.

"Section II. Any person who shall himself, or in combination with any other person or persons, commit either of the offences described in the first section of this act, shall be guilty of a misdemeanor.

"Section III. [This provides a punishment for persons convicted under the above sections by imprisonment in the county jail, not exceeding one year, or by fine not exceeding $250, or by both such fine and imprisonment.]

"Section IV. This act shall take effect immediately."

The primary object of the introduction of this bill was the breaking up of the Moulders' and Machinists' and Blacksmiths' Union in New York State, but its provisions were such that, had it become a law, every trade organization in New York would have been crushed out of existence.

But the workingmen of New York recognized the danger that threatened them. The introduction of that bill in the Legislature provoked among the entire working class of the State such widespread resentment as had seldom been seen. In countless meetings all over the State they protested so resolutely against this bill that the legislators did not dare to pass it and declined to entertain it.

A similar bill was introduced in the Legislature of Massachusetts and passed by one of its houses. But, as in New York, the workingmen of Massachusetts were aroused. In a great demonstration the workingmen of Boston opposed the bill, with the result that it was buried in one of the legislative committees. That the laws of the State should impede or paralyze all attempts to improve their lot was frustrated by the vigilance of the workingmen.

3. Military Interference in Labor Troubles.

The young American bourgeoisie were not satisfied with enlisting in its fight against the rising labor movement, their own economic power and that of the legislature, but they also pressed into their service the military forces and employed the army which had lately been fighting Negro slavery to fortify the slavery of the white workingmen.

On the tenth day of March, 1864, a strike took place among the laborers at Cold Springs, N. Y. These men were in the employ of R. P. Parrott, who was engaged in the manufacture of shot, shell, etc., for the Government. The men were receiving from a dollar to a dollar and a quarter a day. Owing to the very large advance in the prices of all the necessaries of life, they made the request that their wages should be advanced to a dollar and a half a day. This was refused, and a strike was the consequence. Two days after the strike took place, four of the strikers were arrested and sent to Fort Lafayette, where they remained for seven weeks, when they were liberated without a trial, although a trial was demanded. Two companies of United States soldiers were ordered to Cold Springs and martial law was proclaimed, and the men forced to resume work at the old prices. Three of these poor men, who were robbed of seven weeks of their time, and confined in prison for no offence other than exercising their right to refuse to work at a lower price than they were pleased to ask— were not permitted to return to their homes, were driven from their abiding places, exiled in a free land, and their families forced from the town.*

Even worse than in the North was the state of things towards the Southern border line, where martial law had superseded civil law. In St. Louis, in April, 1864, two strikes occurred, one by the tailors, the other by the machinists and blacksmiths As, in part at least, the production of articles used in equipping the army was involved in this strike, the capitalists of the city saw in it a good chance to bring the working-men to terms. On the strength of martial law they demanded military interference in the strike on the part of the commanding general of the district, and their request was but too readily complied with. On the twenty-ninth day of April, 1864, the following order was issued: "General Order No. 65.

"Headquarters Department of the State of
Missouri,
"St. Louis, April 26, 1864.
"It having come to the knowledge of the Commanding General that combinations exist in the

---

* Sylvis, pp. 137-138.

city of St. Louis, having for their object to prevent journeymen mechanics, apprentices and laborers, from working in manufacturing establishments, except on terms prescribed to the proprietors thereof by parties not interested therein,
which terms have no relation to the matter of
wages to be paid to employees, but to the internal
management of such establishments; and it ap-
pearing that, in consequence of such combinations and the practices of those concerned in
them, the operations of some establishments
where articles are produced which are required
for use in the navigation of the Western waters,
and in the military, naval and transport service
of the United States, have been broken up, and
the production of such articles stopped or suspended; the following order is promulgated.
Any violation thereof will be punished as a military offence:

"I. No person shall, directly or indirectly, attempt to deter or prevent any other person from
working on such terms as he may agree upon in
any maunfacturing establishment where any article is ordinarily made which may be required
for use in the navigation of the Western waters,
or in the military, naval or transport service of
the United States.

"II. No person shall watch around or hang
about any such establishment for the purpose of

annoying employees thereof, or learning who are employed therein.

"III. No association or combination shall be formed or continued, or meeting be held, having for its object to prescribe to the proprietors of any such establishment whom they shall employ therein, or how they shall conduct the operation thereof.

"IV. All employees in such establishment will be protected by military authority against all attempts by any person to interfere with or annoy them in their work, or in consequence of their being engaged in it.

"V. The proprietors of every such establishment in the county of St. Louis will forthwith transmit to the office of the Provost-Marshal General the names of all persons who have, since the 15th day of March, 1864, left their employ to engage in any such combination or association as that above referred to; or have been induced to leave by the operations of any such combination or association, or by the individual efforts concerned therein. The places of residence of such persons, as far as known, will be stated, together with a list, by name, of all who have taken an active part in any combination or effort to control the conduct of any such establishment, or to prevent persons from working therein.

"VI. The port commander, Colonel J. H. Baker, 10th Minnesota Volunteers, is charged

under the direction of the district commander
with the execution of this order. All persons ap-
plying for the aid of the military forces in this
connection will report direct to Colonel Baker.

"VII. In putting down this attack upon private rights and the military power of the nation
by organizations led by bad men, the General
confidently relies upon the support and aid of the
city authorities, and of all right-minded men.

"By command of Major-General Rosecrans.

"*O. D. Greene,*
         Assistant Adjutant General.
"*Frank Eno,*
         Assistant Adjutant General."

Several members of the two unions concerned
were arrested, and an intense excitement of the
workers of St. Louis, silent, to be sure, but none
the less intense on that account, was the result.
A demonstration by the workingmen against this
invasion of their rights could not be made, because the city was ruled by martial law. A petition, numerously signed, asking for a modification of the order, was presented to the General,
but without effect.*

A month later exactly similar occurrences took
place in Louisville, Ky. Here, too, there was a
strike, and Brigadier-General Burbridge issued
an order literally identical with the one in St.
Louis, making an end to the efforts of the work-

---

* Sylvis, p. 135.

ingmen to better their condition. It was openly
charged against General Burbridge that he "was
in the confidence of the employers, aware of their
plans and objects, and that he was actuated by
the most selfish and dishonorable motives."*

Sylvis, who discussed all these cases in a
speech, in January, 1865, at the convention of his
trade organization, concluded with the remark
that he had "selected these cases from among
many, such as the breaking up of the Miners'
Association, in the Eastern coal fields, by government interference; the defeat of the Reading
Railroad engineers by the same means; the confiscation of the back pay of the moulders in the
Brooklyn Navy Yard, who struck for higher
wages."†

From out of the midst of the working class
only scattered voices were raised in protest
against this exhibition of violence on the part
of the Government. The organization of labor
was still in its infancy and far too weak and
vague to take a determined stand against these
abuses of authority. It was but natural that in
the course of the Civil War every step which had
the appearance of being against the Government
in Washington was interpreted as a step hostile
to the Union, as a menace to its preservation, as
an encouragement of the rebellious South.

---

* Sylvis, p. 137.
  † Sylvis, p. 140.

Every move of the workingmen which in any way discommoded the Government was branded by the ruling class of the North as treason against the country; and as every attempt of the workingmen was regarded by this class as a molestation of the Government, they denounced every independent act, especially every attempt to secure higher wages and shorter hours, which threatened to disturb the customary course of things, as an act of hostility against the Union. This state of things had to be carefully considered by the workingmen in their organization, their struggles and their demands. It was probably owing to these circumstances that Sylvis, among others, was willing to exculpate the Administration, as most likely not well informed in the matter, from responsibility for the abuse of military power in regard to labor troubles.

Sylvis, moreover, pointed to the fact that the working class of the country had proved their loyalty to the Union during the entire course of the war. He said:

"I presume it is hardly necessary for me to enter into any arguments to prove that the workingmen, the great body of the people, the bone and muscle of the nation, the very pillars of our temple of liberty, are loyal; that, I take it, would be sheer mockery, would be adding insult to injury: for the evidences of our loyalty we need only point to the history of the war; to the fact, that while armed treason and rebellion threatened our institutions with destruction, while the proud and opulent of the land were plotting the downfall of our Government, the toiling millions stood like a wall of adamant between it and the destructive element of revolution, between the country and all its foes."*

But while Sylvis emphasized the loyalty of the working class of the North towards the Union, his remarks left no doubt that the invasions of the capitalists and their Government upon the workingmen had bred a profound irritation in their ranks. He declared:

"These outrages upon the rights of the people have created a profound sensation, have made impressions that can never be erased. It is true that the muttering thunders of the confined volcano were scarcely audible above the surface, but they were none the less deep because in secret."†

The workingmen had not hitherto resented the haughty treatment to which the ruling classes were subjecting them, and Sylvis showed beyond a doubt that this was due exclusively to the exceptional circumstances then prevailing. "Let those," he explained, "who would trample under foot the rights of the working people of this nation, beware. I have wished to show to the country, and especially to those in authority, how

* Sylvis, p. 140.
† Sylvis, pp. 140-141.

near we have been to scenes that would appall
the stoutest heart. In ordinary times a collision
would have been inevitable; nothing but the pa-
triotism of the people, and their desire in no way
to embarrass the Government, prevented it. But
'there is a point where forbearance ceases to be
a virtue,'—that point *may* be reached."*

And in another place Sylvis declares:

"If the doctrines and principles promulgated
and taught by the advocates of union among
workingmen, and the efforts of those engaged in
this movement to secure to labor the fruits of its
toil, and the full enjoyment of all the blessings of
an enlightened civilization, will produce a collision, let it come."†

We note that the conflict between the interests
of the working class and the interests of the agitation in behalf of Negro emancipation which
made itself felt at the inception of the Abolitionist movement, and which is traceable throughout
the entire course of the movement for the abolition of Negro slavery, was still in evidence when
force took command of things, and the bloody
struggle filled the last page of the history of this
movement. And as it is a glorious page in the
history of American workingmen that notwithstanding this conflict of interests they nevertheless on the whole always supported the demand

* Sylvis, p. 141.
† Sylvis, p. 131.

for the abolition of Negro slavery, and that although they lacked the insight of the historic necessity of the abolition of Negro slavery as a condition precedent to their own emancipation, they never failed to regard slavery as a blot on their country; so it is also a glorious page in their history that notwithstanding the most outrageous provocation on the part of the ruling class and the Government during the Civil War, they never wavered in exalting the cause of the Union over their own cause and their class interests. The United States owes it in a large measure to the attitude of the working class that it passed the crisis in those dark days with comparative ease.

4. WHITE SLAVERY.

The war closed after Lincoln had died by the assassin's hand. Negro slavery had ceased to exist. But the close of the war for Negro emancipation was followed by a state of things which the white workingmen of the North could not feel otherwise than as a state of aggravated white slavery.

After the close of the war more than a million men returned to the labor market. Wages were still paid in paper currency, while the price of commodities was fixed by the gold standard. With a gold rate of 153 at the end of the war, $3 in wages was equivalent to only $2 before the war. Despite the apparent increase in wages the workingman was comparatively worse off in 1865 than in 1860. The price of flour, which in 1860 was from $6 to $8 per barrel, had risen in 1865 from $16 to $20 per barrel. Meat had risen from three to four times its price before the war. Previous to 1860 one could buy more with $1 than with $3 six years later.*

During the war at least there had been no dearth of work, because the labor market was not overcrowded. But now that the army of soldiers had largely again changed into an army of workers, the labor market became so glutted that large numbers of workingmen were unable to secure employment. Notwithstanding the prevailing high prices, wages were reduced, so that in the labor world the need of a stronger organization and of new weapons in the impending struggle began to make itself felt.

The attempt was made to establish new connections between the workingmen of the North and those of the South. The national organizations of the printers, the iron founders, the blacksmiths and machinists, had had branches in the Southern States before the war, which were to be revived. Richard F. Trevellick, of Detroit, President of the Shipbuilders' Union, was sent to organize new unions. But for the time being his efforts were futile; for the moment no labor

* *National Workman.* New York, 1866.

movement was to be thought of in the land of the emancipated slaves.

In August, 1866, Northern workingmen met at a convention in Baltimore which gave a new impulse to the eight-hour movement and which witnessed the foundation of the National Labor Union. A lively agitation was inaugurated for shorter hours, which in 1868 led to the passage in Congress of an eight-hour law, signed by President Johnson.

The American workingmen of the North had not hitherto entered into any relations with the International Workingmen's Association, whose General Council in London, during the Civil War, had so powerfully championed the interests of the Union and persuaded the working class of Europe, and especially of England, to oppose all plots on the part of the ruling class in behalf of the Southern rebels. In the first years of its existence the International met with scant attention on the part of the American workingmen. The war absorbed all their energies, and the labor movement of the country was as yet too loosely rooted to feel a desire of getting into touch with foreign workingmen.

But immediately after the Baltimore convention the leaders of the American labor movement turned their eyes towards London, intent on establishing closer relations between the American and the English labor movements. On October

13, 1866, there appeared in New York the first issue of a weekly labor paper, called *The National Workman* and devoted "to the interests of the working classes." This paper, which was published by a man named Jones, contained good reports of the state of the current labor movement. Its platform consisted of the resolutions adopted by the Baltimore convention; it went even beyond them by forcibly impressing the workingmen with the need of independent political action. With its twelfth issue the paper was made the official organ of the central labor body of New York. It was also the organ of the Workingmen's Assembly, the annual meeting of all labor organizations of the State. Unfortunately *The National Workman* lived but a short time. Its last issue appeared on March 2, 1867.

This paper was the first in America to direct the attention of its readers to the International Workingmen's Association. *The National Workman* reported not only the proceedings of the Association at the Geneva Congress, but occasionally it also published reports of the meetings of the General Council in London and the resolutions passed there. W. I. Jessup, a ship carpenter, who had been exceedingly active during the Civil War in his trade union, was connected with it. Immediately after the Baltimore convention, Jessup appealed to the general secretary of the Society of Carpenters and Joiners in London to assist in establishing regular communication between the American and the English carpenters' and joiners' organizations. In a letter dated October 14, 1866, the general secretary of the joiners of London, Robert Applegarth,* gladly agreed to the proposition and at the same time sent Jessup a number of documents, adding the words:

"I have to ask: is it not possible to amalgamate your body with ours? The Amalgamated Society of Engineers have set us the example. Why not follow it? They have branches at Bloomington, Ill., Buffalo and Dunkirk, N. Y., Susquehanna, Pa., and in New York City."

Robert Applegarth was a member of the General Council of the International Workingmen's Association, and we may assume that his relations with Jessup, who in turn was in communication with Sylvis, gave rise to the epistolary exchange of ideas which now followed between Sylvis and the General Council of the International.

At the second convention of the National Labor Union in Chicago in 1867 Jessup and Sylvis advocated an official alliance between this American workingmen's organization and the International Workingmen's Association. They did not

---

* In *The National Workman* which published this letter the name is erroneously spelled Applegate.

succeed in effecting it, but the following resolution was passed:

"Whereas, The efforts of the working classes of Europe to secure the political power in order to improve their social and other conditions, and to throw off the bondage in which they have been and are still held, furnish satisfactory testimony of the progress of justice, culture and humanity;

"Be it resolved, That the National Labor Union in convention assembled, hereby assure the organized workingmen of Europe of their sympathy and co-operation in the struggle against political and social injustice."

Although the National Labor Union of America did not officially join the International Workingmen's Association, Sylvis continued to, communicate with the General Council.

In the spring of 1869 the tension between the United States and England, which had been produced by the latter's unfriendly attitude during the Civil War, reached such a degree as to make imminent a war between the two countries. The General Council of the International resolved to oppose the prevailing war sentiment, and to this end sent an address to Sylvis, as the president of the National Labor Union, in which the working class of America was exhorted by its attitude to counteract the war cry of the ruling classes and to stand for the preservation of peace. This ad-

dress, which was dated May 12, 1869, read as
follows:

"Fellow Workmen:

"In the inaugural address of our Association
we said: 'It was not the wisdom of the ruling
classes, but the heroic resistance to their criminal
folly by the working classes of England that
saved the West of Europe from plunging head-
long into an infamous crusade for the perpetuation and propagation of slavery on the other side
of the Atlantic.' It is now your turn to prevent
a war whose direct result would be to throw
back, for an indefinite period, the rising labor
movement on both sides of the Atlantic.

"We need hardly tell you that there are
European powers anxiously engaged in foment-
ing a war between the United States and England. A glance at the statistics of commerce
shows that the Russian export of raw products
—and Russia has nothing else to export—was
giving way to American competition when the
Civil War tipped the scales. To turn the American ploughshare into a sword would at this time
save from impending bankruptcy a power whom
your republican statesmen in their wisdom had
chosen for their confidential adviser. But disregarding the particular interests of this or that
government, is it not in the general interest of
our oppressors to disturb by a war the move-

ment of rapidly extending international co-operation?

"In our congratulatory address to Mr. Lincoln on the occasion of his re-election to the Presidency we expressed it as our conviction that the Civil War would prove to be as important to the progress of the working class as the War of Independence has been to the elevation of the middle class. And the successful close of the war against slavery has indeed inaugurated a new era in the annals of the working class. In the United States itself an independent labor movement has since arisen which the old parties and the professional politicians view with distrust. But to bear fruit it needs years of peace. To suppress it, a war between the United States and England would be the sure means.

"The immediate tangible result of the Civil War was of course a deterioration of the condition of American workingmen. Both in the United States and in Europe the colossal burden of a public debt was shifted from hand to hand in order to settle it upon the shoulders of the working class. The prices of necessaries, remarks one of your statesmen, have risen 78 per cent. since 1860, while the wages of simple manual labor have risen 50 and those of skilled labor 60 per cent. 'Pauperism,' he complains, 'is increasing in America more rapidly than population.' Moreover the sufferings of the working class are in glaring contrast to the new-fangled luxury of financial aristocrats, shoddy aristocrats and other vermin bred by war. Still the Civil War offered a compensation in the liberation of the slaves and the impulse which it thereby gave to your own class movement. Another war, not sanctified by a sublime aim or a social necessity, but like the wars of the Old World, would forge chains for the free workingmen instead of sundering those of the slave. The accumulated misery which it would leave in its wake would furnish your capitalists at once with the motive and the means of separating the working class from their courageous and just aspirations by the soulless sword of a standing army. Yours, then, is the glorious task of seeing to it that at last the working class shall enter upon the scene of history, no longer as a servile following, but as an independent power, as a power imbued with a sense of its responsibility and capable of commanding peace where their would-be masters cry war.

"In the name of the International Workingmen's Association.

"For Great Britain: R. Applegarth, carpenter; M. D. Brown, mechanic; J. Buckley, painter; J. Hales, rubber weaver; Harriet Law; B. Lucraft, chairmaker; J. Milner, tailor; G. Odger, shoemaker; J. Ross, bootlegmaker; R. Shaw, painter;

Cowell Stepney; J. Warren, satchelmaker; J. Weston, bannistermaker.

"For France: E. Dupont, instrument maker; Jules Johannard, Paul Lafargue.

"For Germany: J. G. Eccarius, tailor; F. Lessner, tailor; W. Limburg, shoemaker; Karl Marx.

"For Switzerland: H. Jung, watchmaker; A. Müller, watchmaker.

"For Belgium: P. Bernard, painter.

"For Denmark: I. Cohn, cigarmaker.

"For Poland: A. Idbricki, compositor.

> "BENJAMIN LUCRAFT, President.
>
> "COWELL STEPNEY, Treasurer.
>
> "J. GEORG ECCARIUS,
>
> General Secretary.

"London, May 12th, 1869."

Sylvis, as president of the National Labor Union, made the following acknowledgment of the receipt of this Address to the General Council of the International Workingmen's Association:

> "Philadelphia, May 26, 1869.

"Your letter of the 12th instant, together with the Address, came to hand yesterday; I am pleased to get such kind words from fellow-workmen on the other side of the ocean. We have a common cause. It is the war of poverty against wealth. In all parts of the world labor occupies the same lowly position, capital is everywhere the same tyrant. Therefore I say we have a com-

mon cause. In the name of the workingmen of
the United States, I extend to you, and through
you to all those whom you represent, and to all
the downtrodden and oppressed sons and daughters of labor in Europe the right hand of
fellowship. Continue in the good work that
you have undertaken, until a glorious success shall crown your efforts! Such is our re-
solve. Our recent war has led to the foundation
of the most infamous money aristocracy of the
earth. This money power saps the very life of
the people. We have declared war against it and
we are determined to conquer—by means of the
ballot, if possible—if not, we shall resort to more
serious means. A little blood-letting is necessary in desperate cases."

The Address of the General Council of the International to the American workingmen urging
them to oppose a war with England was the last
manifestation of this body relating to the North
American struggles and their consequences grow-
ing out of Negro slavery.

The economic disadvantage which the Civil
War imposed upon the American workingmen
caused the latter for many years yet to ponder
the subject of slavery, and to institute com-
parisons between the prevailing white slavery and
the black slavery that had been abolished. In a
speech delivered by Sylvis in September, 1868,

at Sunbury, Pa., these two kinds of slavery were referred to in the following comments:

"Within the last seven years we have passed through the most gigantic war the world ever saw—a rebellion such as no other government could have successfully combated. Whatever our opinions may be as to immediate causes of the war, we can all agree that human slavery (property in man) was the first great cause; and from the day that the first gun was fired, it was my earnest hope that the war might not end until slavery ended with it. No man in America rejoiced more than I at the downfall of Negro slavery. But when the shackles fell from the limbs of those four millions of blacks, it did not make them *free* men; it simply transferred them from one condition of slavery to another; it placed them upon the platform of the white workingmen, and made all slaves together. I do not mean that freeing the Negro enslaved the white; I mean that we were slaves before, always have been, and that the abolition of the right of property in man added four millions of black slaves to the white slaves of the country. We are now all one family of slaves together, and the labor reform movement is a second emancipation proclamation."*

And shortly thereafter, on November 16, 1868, Sylvis declared in a circular published by him:

* Sylvis, p. 232 ff.

"Our people are being divided into two classes
—the rich and the poor, the producers and the
non-producers; the busy bees in the industrial
hive, and the idle drones who fatten upon what
they steal. The working-people of our nation,
white and black, male and female, are sinking to
a condition of serfdom. Even now a slavery
exists in our land worse than ever existed under
the old slave system."*

Negro slavery was put down on the bloody
battlefields of the South, in no small degree, as
we have seen, by the assistance of the very workingmen who had reason to complain of the white
slavery under which they groaned. But their
own slavery they have not yet been able to put
down. History does not proceed by leaps and
bounds, and as the time had to be ripe and the
way had to be cleared by economic development
for the abolition of Negro slavery, so the time
will have to be ripe and the way will have to be
cleared by economic development for the
abolition of wage slavery.

Will the bloody spectacle be repeated on a
larger scale—the bloody spectacle of the
struggles for the emancipation of the slaves and
the restoration of the Union in the years from

* Sylvis, p. 82.

1861 to 1865? Will the peaceful and orderly
victory of the working class at the polls—an
event as sure to occur as was the victory of the
Republican party in 1860—be followed by armed
revolt on the part of the industrial overlords and
their conscripts? Will they, as did the slaveholders of 1860, strive to disrupt the Union and
to overthrow popular government? One is almost tempted to believe it when one considers the
bearing of the ruling classes who, stubborn and
haughty as the Southern oligarchy in the past,
oppose all change in the constitution of society
and refuse to yield even the least of their privileges. But then a nation which has lived through
one such crisis may be expected to guard against
its repetition.